ROLE

SOCIOLOGICAL STUDIES 4

Role

EDITED BY

J. A. JACKSON

*Professor of Social Theory and
Institutions, Queen's University
Belfast*

CAMBRIDGE at the University Press 1972

Published by the Syndics of the Cambridge University Press
Bentley House, 200 Euston Road, London NW1 2DB
American Branch: 32 East 57th Street, New York, N.Y.10022

© Cambridge University Press 1972

Library of Congress Catalogue Card Number: 70-164451

I S B N : 0 521 08307 9

Printed in Great Britain
by W. Heffer & Sons Ltd.

EDITOR'S PREFACE

The concept of role has been central to the development of knowledge about, and measures of, the normative context which mediates between the individual and society. The whole controversy of the primacy of 'nature' or 'nurture' has been contained within this loose-fitting concept of role. On the one hand it depends on dramatic analogy — 'a man plays many parts'; on the other it represents the total sum of socialized human personality responding to the defined needs of specific, structured situations. It is not a happy concept in that it lacks precise meaning and its empirical reference is necessarily rather indirect.

As in the first three numbers on *Social Stratification, Migration* and *Professions and Professionalization* the purpose of this volume is to raise a number of questions about the adequacy of theoretical concepts used by sociologists and others to describe social phenomena. In particular the adequacy of concepts that have 'passed into the literature' needs constantly to be reassessed in terms of new research findings and varying empirical examples. The editorial aim of the series is not, however, to provide a new 'final' statement in the form of a 'reader' or a set of papers which tidy up the theoretical garden.

In the best sense it is hoped that Sociological Studies will provide *working papers* on a theme of general and continuing interest to social scientists rather than final statements. The international range covered by the contributors together with the intention that they should speculate freely on the problem produces inevitable discrepancies of viewpoint and highlights further problems yet to be resolved. Equally it is hoped that the series will continue to provide, as it has in its initial volumes, a forum for the development and furthering of contemporary theory in the social sciences as this develops from varying traditions and with differing national tendencies and interests.

With the exception of the paper by Professor Heinrich Popitz, which appears for the first time in English translation, each paper has been specially written for this volume. I am grateful to Professor Popitz and his publishers, J. C. B. Mohr (Paul Siebeck) of Tübingen, for permission to translate and reproduce *Der Begriff der Sozialen Rolle als Element der Soziologischen Theorie.*

Sociological Studies 5 will be devoted to the theme of 'Social Change' and will appear in 1972.

J.A.J.

Belfast
March 1971

CONTRIBUTORS

Malcolm Bradbury
Professor of American Literature, University of East Anglia

Margaret Coulson
Senior Lecturer in Sociology, Harris College, Preston

Chad Gordon
Fox Professor of Sociology, Rice University, Texas

Bryan Heading
Lecturer in Sociology, University of East Anglia

Martin Hollis
Lecturer in Philosophy, University of East Anglia

Heinrich Popitz
Professor of Sociology, University of Marburg

W. G. Runciman

John Urry
Lecturer in Sociology, University of Lancaster

CONTENTS

1

ROLE—EDITORIAL INTRODUCTION

JOHN A. JACKSON

I

Georg Simmel asked in the title to a famous essay 'How is society possible?'[1] The conventional answer for his sociological successors, especially those who have neglected to read him, has been found in the concept of role. Indeed, one of the more surprising features of the intellectual history of contemporary sociology is the degree to which this elusive concept has been taken for granted by its users as a kind of theoretical haven where they could rest on their intellectual laurels while struggling with the more tractable problems of the discipline. By using role to define 'How sociology is possible' many of the fundamental dilemmas raised by abstraction in sociology, and in particular those indissolubly linked abstractions, individual and society, can be set on one side.

In most introductory texts the student will be introduced to role as one of the basic concepts of the discipline. He will learn that social roles or positions are filled by individuals who perform in them more or less adequately. The normative constraints of society are thus tangibly represented in a system of roles for performance in which the individual is socialized, which subsequently define his rights, privileges and social relationships. Such students, particularly if these textbooks have been written within the American tradition, will then be led to consider the substantive areas of socialization, normative control and deviant behaviour and institutional role complexes such as family, occupation or religion. They are less likely to return, at least in their first year's work, to the broader philosophical issues concealed within the apparently innocent Pandora's box labelled 'role'.

The European tradition has rested more on the fundamental problems of the nature of society, 'the theory of society' rather than 'sociological theory', and has in recent years been most clearly developed within Germany and especially in the definition of 'critical sociology' developed by Habermas and others.[2] As Dahrendorf suggests in introducing a recent collection of essays, 'A theory of society, then, not only prepares the way for the formulation of sociological theories, but accompanies such theories as a guard against their reification and a reminder of their implications, both theoretical and practical.'[3]

---

[1] G. Simmel, 'How is society possible?', *American Journal of Sociology,* vol. 16, 3, 1910/11, pp. 372-91.

[2] J. Habermas, *Theorie und Praxis: Sozialphilosophische Studien* (Neuwied-Berlin, 1963).

[3] R. Dahrendorf, *Essays in the Theory of Society* (London, 1968), p. vii.

Precisely because of the need for sociologists to demonstrate the initial reality of 'society' the concept of role has been readily and uncritically reified in this sense. It has been absorbed as a primary sociological abstraction, essential to understanding the social bond and the social fabric, conveniently articulating society as external normative constraints in Durkheim's sense, with the individual as an immanent actor in a socially prescribed part. This primary sociological abstraction tends then, too often, to be swallowed whole without there being much attempt to explore fully its conceptual strengths and weaknesses, its explanatory value or its possibilities of empirical verification. 'Role theory' has tended to be concerned more with one side or the other of the abstraction; it has emphasized personality in relation to social psychology or functional normative constraints in relation to deviance and conformity. Even a recent text by Michael Banton with the title *Roles* and attempting to use the concept as a major explanatory device enjoins its readers to the necessity for a truce: 'It is necessary to assume in the examination of particular roles that there is agreement among all the parties affected as to the definition of the role in question.'[1] As Heinrich Popitz points out in the paper included in this volume, the concept of social role is 'progenitive of, and almost simultaneously fatal to, sociological detachment'.[2]

The most significant debate surrounding the concept in recent years developed in Germany in response to the publication of Ralf Dahrendorf's 'Homo Sociologicus: or the history, significance, and limits of the category of social role' in 1958. In reality this has been a debate about the nature of sociology itself and has been instructive for the extent to which it focussed attention on the assumptions on which the concept was based. Dahrendorf in a Postscript to 'Homo Sociologicus', 'Sociology and Human Nature', published in 1962, reiterates this point characteristically: 'To put the matter paradoxically, at the risk of being misunderstood: even if sociology asks questions about man, it is in substance concerned not with man but with ways of reducing man's actions to rational terms.'[3]

Without misunderstanding Dahrendorf's assumptions here, it is, of course, precisely the kinds of rationality to which those actions have been reduced, that have created the arid, dehumanized and rigid characteristics of *homo sociologicus* especially in some of his earlier and more deterministic variants. The notion of role, however used, depends then on certain assumptions regarding the nature of man, his plasticity as a learner, his capacity in reflecting the expectations of others, his criteria of rationality, and his perception of situations in terms of his interests. In using the notion of role as a sociological abstraction of the conditions of human behaviour we should necessarily define these limits with some precision if *homo sociologicus*, 'role player', is to be an abstraction of man rather than mask.

1   M. Banton, *Roles: an Introduction to the Study of Social Relations* (London, 1965), p. 36.
2   See below, H. Popitz, 'The concept of social role as an element of sociological theory', p. 11.
3   R. Dahrendorf, 'Sociology and human nature', *Theory of Society,* pp. 94-5.

II

The variety of usages to which the concept of role is put further demonstrates its uncertain status within general sociological theory. Essentially it rests on the analogy with the theatre, a dimension to be discussed more fully below; it is a part, a character played out in accordance with the expectations of an audience. Indeed it is a part corresponding to a defined social position the incumbent of which is expected to behave in predictable ways. It is precisely on the basis of such predictions regarding the (normal) behaviour of fathers to sons, masters to servants, husbands to wives, that the possibility of enduring social relationships rests. The problem, of course, with the dramaturgical analogy lies in the fact that the lines for the part appear to have been lost. If society is the playwright then how is the actor to learn his part perfectly and to what extent is it assumed that he can and must *ad lib*?

Some recognition of the dilemma is usually found in the paired sets of definitions used to distinguish the dual components of role. Linton for instance uses status to define an ideal pattern of conduct, and role to define actual behaviour; Parsons distinguishes status with reference to obligations, and role as denoting rights;[1] Nadel distinguishes between 'status' and 'person'.[2] Banton in his definition of role suggests that while we may define it as 'a set of norms and expectations applied to the incumbent of a particular position' we must continue to recognize two distinct approaches to it. 'A psychological approach is likely to concentrate upon how these ideas are held by individuals. The structural approach traces the way the sharing of norms and expectations creates networks of rights and obligations'.[3] Rather more precise formulations of the definitions of role are to be found in the work of Merton, Gross and others who have moved beyond the level of simple and arbitrary definition to the more solid problems of 'role-complexes', 'role-sets', 'role-clusters', 'role-consistency' and 'role-conflict' and have paid attention to the relationship of subjective role definition to reference group theory.

It is indeed progress to have moved away from the too simple and arbitrary definitions of role. 'The concept of role is at present still rather vague, nebulous and non-definitive.'[4] A full definition today demands analytical precision in relation to the component strands which have contributed to the development of 'role-theory', often without reference to one another. Our definition of social role, then, must

1 T. Parsons, *The Social System* (Glencoe, Ill., 1951). In a more recent essay Parsons defines role in the following terms: 'But since the typical individual participates in more than one collectivity, the relevant structural unit is not the "total" individual or personality, but the individual as a role. In its normative aspect, then, a role may be thought of as the system of normative expectations for the performance of a participating individual in his capacity as a member of a collectivity. The role is the primary point of direct articulation between the personality of the individual and the structure of the social system.' *Sociological Theory and Modern Society* (New York, 1967).
2 S. F. Nadel, *The Theory of Social Structure* (London, 1957).
3 M. Banton, *Roles*, p. 29.
4 L. J. Neimann and J. W. Hughes, 'The problem of the concept of role – a re-survey of the literature', *Social Forces*, 30 (1951), p. 149.

endeavour to bridge these divergent component traditions as well as recognizing the fundamental tension between subjective and objective elements, between individual and society represented in the human paradox.

One strand in the tradition of role theory derives from Cooley's notion of the 'looking-glass self',[1] Mead's 'taking the role of the other', via Piaget's theory of the stages of development and infant socialization[2] to the more refined social psychology of Theodore Newcomb[3] and Biddle and Thomas.[4] It has been developed as a component of the discussion of the relationship between nature and nurture, the socialization process and the characteristic attributes of personality formation. The emphasis on socialization within this tradition has perhaps tended to place stress on 'preparation for adult roles' and to give rise to assumptions about the relatively fixed social positions for adequate performance in which the whole socialization experience is a necessary preparation. Ineffective adult role-performance, deviance, differential aspiration, etc. could then, in part at least, be attributed to failures or dissonances in the maturation process by which ideally stages of physical development were linked to the appropriate levels of socialization and transition.

A second tradition has emphasized the structural components of societies and has tended to consider the structural or functional requirements of societies as the defining set of constraints (obligations and rights) which govern individuals occupying different positions in society. The set of assumptions underlying this tradition has been based, at least originally, on simple societies, or at least those in which social positions appeared relatively fixed and constant. Role was then used to describe the extent to which individual behaviour actually corresponded to the ideal, and the paired concepts of status and role were thus used in an attempt to distinguish the ideal and the actual elements of behaviour in relation to a functional (and essentially static) model of society. Two concepts have not fared much better than one in the sense that the distinction has been neither always precise nor consistent enough to make any substantial analytic contribution to the discussion. The term status has, in any case, increasingly been limited to its proper reference to positions within a social stratification system and has only a limited utility in relation to the general theory of role.[5] Broadly, though one may suggest that this

1 C. H. Cooley, *Human Nature and the Social Order* (New York, 1902).
2 J. Piaget, *The Language and Thought of the Child* (New York, 1955), and G. H. Mead, *Mind, Self and Society* (Chicago, 1934). See also A. Strauss (ed.), *The Social Psychology of George Herbert Mead* (Chicago, 1956).
3 T. Newcomb, *Social Psychology* (New York, 1950).
4 B. J. Biddle and E. H. Thomas (eds.), *Role Theory: Concepts and Research* (New York, 1966).
5 The conceptual tangles surrounding the use of the term status have been well summarized by Alvin Gouldner who, after an extensive list of definitions, concludes: 'That these varying definitions are not necessarily contradictory is small consolation and certainly no guarantee that they all refer to the same things. Nowhere do these definitions become more opaque than when – as they frequently do – they refer to a status as a "position" in something. The ready familiarity of the word "position" seems to induce paralysis of the analytic nerve.' Alvin V. Gouldner, 'Cosmopolitans and locals: toward an analysis of latent social roles – I', *Administrative Science Quarterly*, 2 (December 1957), 284.

tradition has tended to emphasize a model of society in which the functional division of labour has developed to produce a category of roles on which universal conclusions can be based, one must doubt that the dependence on status as the referent for role and role performance is necessarily productive. There is a status for wife but is there a status, in the same sense, for woman? In other words the level of specificity tends to characterize the real utility of the status–role relationship.

In any case it is precisely in these areas of relatively unstructured social interactions – the garden so richly cultivated by Simmel,[1] Goffman[2] and Aubert[3] among others – that the relationship of role to fixed position or status breaks down. The management of identity in 'confined', 'open' or 'abnormal' situations calls for an analysis of social action and interaction less contained than the characteristically institutionalized 'theatre' which role-theory habitually provides for. Popitz points out in his paper the 'characteristic' quality of such roles and, following Weber's analysis of legitimation of authority structures, shows how leadership roles emerge from recognition and response, e.g. institutionalization on the part of an audience. 'The decisive fact is whether a position can develop whose rights and duties can be exercized not just by one individual in his uniqueness. Only with the de-individualization of norms are role-norms formed.'[4]

III

The difficulties and weaknesses of general role theory are discussed fully in the papers which follow and for many of the reasons already hinted at in this brief introductory discussion doubts are raised about the concept and its usage as a general proposition in sociology. While in more than one paper it is suggested that we should abandon the concept altogether, it is precisely because of the ambiguities which attach to it that it is seen as unsatisfactory. In other words most sociologists would readily admit that once one can be precise about the limited area in which one is specifying role characteristics the concept has a demonstrable utility and an analytical precision. It is merely that we must not let the fact that role analysis is a profitable and necessary activity for the sociologist lead us to a too-ready assumption that we have solved the general propositions contained in the concept of role itself. As Gouldner remarked in an important article almost fifteen years ago, 'The very currency of role concepts may invite complacency concerning their theoretical clarity.'[5]

1   K. Woolf (ed.), *The Sociology of Georg Simmel* (New York, 1950).
2   E. Goffman, *The Presentation of Self in Everyday Life* (London, 1969); *Stigma: notes on the management of spoiled identity* (Englewood Cliffs, N.J., 1964); *Encounters* (Indianapolis, 1961); *Strategic Interaction* (Oxford, 1970).
3   V. Aubert, *The Hidden Society* (Totowa, N.J., 1965).
4   See below, H. Popitz, 'The concept of role as an element of sociological theory', p. 17.
5   A. Gouldner, 'Cosmopolitans and locals: toward an analysis of latent social roles', *Administrative Science Quarterly,* 2 (December 1957), 281.

The tendencies toward simplistic determinist analysis of social position and role-occupant has been greatly modified by the emphasis within specific studies of the complexity of role-audiences — the different sets of parties concerned with both the normative constraints and the actual performance. These audiences have been described by Merton as 'role-sets'[1] corresponding to a given occupation — in his case the school teacher. Gross and his colleagues make a similar and far-reaching analysis in relation to the 'role' of school superintendents[2] and the extent of consensus among these 'audiences' of the role in question. Differential perception, role-taking and reference group theory thus introduce an analysis of the context of social action and the capacity for role modification in relation to this context. Basic to the theory of social action as developed by Parsons, such analysis illuminates and defines operationally significant aspects of role which can be usefully developed. Turner, for instance, takes the concept of role-taking as a fundamental aspect of social interaction where it is understood as 'a process of looking at or anticipating another's behavior by viewing it in the context of a role imputed to that other'.[3] The heartland of symbolic criterionist theory is reached in the 'double-bind' of actor responding emphatically to actor in determining his own subsequent action. As Devereux summarizes Parson's theory: 'The minimum frame of reference for talking about action must therefore include, beside the actor and the situation, some explicit reference to subjective processes or orientation, conceived as causally relevant interviewing mechanisms and not as epiphenomena, and to explicitly formulated notions of ends or goals and of normative standards, conceived as ideal elements which function to structure the actor's orientation to situations.'[4]

In her paper in this book Margaret Coulson makes some just and swingeing criticisms of neologistic exercises in sociology. The difficulty is a real one and not one that we can entirely ignore — the concept is as good as it is precise but the attempt at precision leads to 'ever more complicated qualifications and sub-qualifications while the relationship of the theory to the policeman's actual behaviour, for example, becomes ever more remote and unconvincing'.[5] We return to the dilemma with which we started; the nature of the rationality of sociological concepts about human behaviour, whether derived from dramatic analogy, deductive rationality or mechanistic or organic models, remains a construct, a mask which hopefully will reveal rather than entirely conceal the man beneath.

---

1   R. K. Merton, 'The role set', *British Journal of Sociology* (June 1957), 108.
2   N. Gross, W. Mason and A. McEachern, *Exploration in Role Analysis: Studies of the school superintendency role* (London, 1966).
3   Ralph H. Turner, 'Role-taking, role standpoint, and reference group behavior', *American Journal of Sociology*, 61 (January 1956), 316.
4   E. C. Devereux, Jr, 'Parsons' sociological theory', in M. Black (ed.), *The Social Theories of Talcott Parsons* (Englewood Cliffs, N.J., 1961), p. 21.
5   See below, M. Coulson, 'Role: a redundant concept in sociology? Some Educational Considerations', p. 114.

IV

Emerging from the growing and substantial sociological debate on role theory in Germany, Popitz' important paper *Der Begriff der Sozialen Rolle als Element der Soziologischen Theorie* has unfortunately only been available hitherto in a German edition.[1] It represents a substantial analysis of the whole history of role theory and the essential difficulties which have arisen from Linton's early distinctions and which continue in contemporary sociological theory.[2] Though Dahrendorf's 'Homo Sociologicus' essay is now well known outside Germany, Popitz' critique of the necessity for such a stark abstraction is not. In translation it still provides, some five years after its original German publication, a valuable definitive statement about the discussion of role which does much to make the task of the present editor easier in introducing an inevitably diverse set of papers with a variety of approaches to the topic.

The discussion which follows has the form of a dialogue between three of my former colleagues at the University of East Anglia. A number of us from different disciplines had occasion to work together on the frontiers of our various subjects and it seemed opportune that the concept of role, which was certainly part of the professional as well as the commonsense vocabulary of literary criticism, philosophy and sociology, should form the subject of such an exchange. Naturally enough it focusses on the criteria of rational abstraction in deference to Hollis's interest as a philosopher and on the dramaturgical analogy in deference to Bradbury's interest in the theatre. That Heading, as sociologist, is encouraged to face some of the implications and theoretical assumptions surrounding the concept is fruitful. Clearly such a discussion cannot resolve all the problems but it does demonstrate that the somewhat neurotic concerns of sociologists with their intellectual equipment can benefit from debate among a wider circle of colleagues.

Gordon's paper on role development in relation to the stages of the life cycle extends the work of Ralph Turner's comprehensive model and stresses the changing character of roles.[3] Far from being static the basic roles linked to the stages of development are emerging and receding; they are not whole suits of clothes picked out of the prop box to be taken on entire. Starting with an ideal-typical life-cycle model for contemporary, urban, middle-class America, Gordon extends this discussion, stressing the aspects of internalization and institutionalization of the role already noted in relation to the paper by Popitz. The question of identity and

1   H. Popitz, *Der Begriff der Sozialen Rolle als Element der Soziologischen Theorie* (J. C. B. Mohr (Paul Siebeck), Tübingen, 1967).
2   R. H. Linton, *The Study of Man* (New York, 1936), and also a later work in which there is some change in emphasis in his concept of role in relation to status but still some confusion as to the dimensions involved in the dual concept of role in relation to status. In *The Cultural Background of Personality* (New York, 1945), he writes: 'The term role will be used to designate the sum total of the culture patterns associated with a particular status.'
3   See R. H. Turner, 'Role-taking, role standpoint and reference group behaviour', in B. J. Biddle and E. J. Thomas (eds.), *Role Theory*, pp. 151-9.

personal autonomy discussed in connection with retirement and the giving-up of significant roles gives fresh insight into the general question of whether there is a 'person underneath when all the social roles are removed'.

Margaret Coulson questions the continued utility of the concept of role and suggests that it should be abandoned in favour of a more specific and dynamic conceptual framework. She exemplifies this in relation to the situation of the school and makes reference to a number of recent attempts to introduce a conflict model into analysis of the educational setting. It is surprising how frequently education is selected as the arena *par excellence* in discussions of role and role-theory. Merton,[1] Gross,[2] and Elder[3] are only a few of those who have found this a most fruitful field for research and illustration. As a milieu it is, of course, a natural continuation of the life-cycle analysis developed further here in Chad Gordon's paper. Certainly education is an area rich in its fusion of the socialization and maturation process. In addition the parental surrogate roles of teachers demonstrate a conflict in role performance which is further aggravated by uncertainties of professional status.[4] A recent example in Northern Ireland which came to my attention reinforces one such point of role conflict. In a boys' school where the large majority of teachers are male and where it is customary for the boys to refer to them as 'Sir' this mode of address is used by the boys to the women teachers as well. Though one doubts if this is widespread, similar examples, such as the use of husbands' rank and number for wives of servicemen being treated in military hospitals, underline the point, and incidentally suggest that the present movement for 'women's liberation' has a lot of ground to cover.

John Urry's paper provides a critical analysis of the reference group in relation to role theory, its origins in the symbolic interactionist sociological tradition and the failure, in his view, of attempts at applying the concept of comparative reference group. This concept, most signally illustrated by Stouffer's study of the American soldier[5] in 1949, rests on certain assumptions about the process of self-evaluation in relation to others. His paper is primarily concerned with a full critique of this area with particular attention to W. G. Runciman's *Relative Deprivation and Social Justice.*[6] Urry raises both theoretical and methodological difficulties which, he claims, lie in the psychological model on which the theory of social comparison rests as well as the equilibrium theory of society implicit in the relative deprivation hypothesis.

---

1   R. K. Merton, 'The role set'.
2   N. Gross, W. Mason and A. McEachern, *Explorations in Role Analysis.*
3   G. Elder, Jr, 'Age integration and socialization in an educational setting', *Harvard Educational Review,* 37, 4 (1967), 594-619.
4   T. Leggatt, 'Teaching as a profession', in J. A. Jackson (ed.), *Professions and Professionalization* (Cambridge, 1970).
5   S. A. Stouffer *et al., The American Soldier* (New York, 1949).
6   W. G. Runciman, *Relative Deprivation and Social Justice: a Study of Attitudes to Social Inequality in twentieth century England* (London, 1966).

Runciman in the concluding short paper has provided a reply to Urry's criticisms and has developed the discussion further in relation to some of the critical points which Urry raises. The discussion will not rest here; nor should it. As in other branches of role analysis considered earlier there is still much room for debate. In his concluding remarks Runciman reminds us that 'the only justification of theoretical or methodological discussion of this kind is its pay-off in empirical research'.[1] So far there has been all too little to test the validity of the still very generalized concepts surrounding the notion of social role.

---

1   See below, W. G. Runciman, 'Reply to Mr Urry', p. 147.

2

THE CONCEPT OF SOCIAL ROLE AS AN ELEMENT OF SOCIOLOGICAL THEORY

HEINRICH POPITZ

I

Even in sociology the concept of role shows evidence of its origins. Here too it leads a rather dramatic existence.

Role, role-player, role-behaviour; with these words is often connected the first general theoretical abstraction in sociology that is really intelligible to the sociology student. They are obviously particularly suited both to demonstrating social phenomena and, at the same time, to inculcating a way of seeing things at a distance, of rendering remote what is all too close in everyday social experience and of making what is self-evident in social contexts strange. Though the role-concept performs this service without much difficulty it quickly loses its function again: all too speedily it fits into colloquial usage, leads to limitless associations and allows itself to be arbitrarily brought into play. With little effort all social experiences can be 'en-roled'. Thus, the process soon turns full circle: the concept of social role is today progenitive of, and almost simultaneously fatal to, sociological detachment.

The obvious suggestion that another, less easily-misused, word be selected is no longer practicable. Sociology has taken its concepts, to a relatively large extent, from colloquial speech. It was only as a secondary consideration that comparison on an international scale was begun. Mainly those — mostly Latin — words have prevailed which exist with almost the same sound in the major languages: norm, sanction, institution, organization, group, social control, class, status, mobility — and, of course, role. There is practically no choice left now but to delimit and equate further the often very different areas of meaning in the particular languages.

As with all such abstractions one may delve as far back in the history of sociology as one likes if it is desired to show that something similar has always hitherto been 'meant'.[1] It is, however, more instructive to see in the works of Georg Simmel what expenditure of general theoretical reflection was necessary — how far

---

1 Thus in his polemic against Plato, Aristotle points out the variety and relativity of 'role-norms' in order to emphasize their independence, as against their dissolution by Plato in the general concept of virtue. The virtue of the good citizen is not simply the virtue of a good man; it corresponds at any given time to his particular position and task in the polis, and changes as the constitutions change. Even for slaves there is a specific virtue, just as for husband and wife, adult and child. See the interpretation in Lothar Philipps, *Zur Ontologie der sozialen Rolle* (Frankfurt am Main, 1963), pp. 37ff.

he had to dig down, in order to find the decisive points of view. Yet here, too, they are still not set down sufficiently unequivocally. Only later, in Anglo-Saxon social anthropology, does there develop out of the problems of relativity in cultural comparison that interest for formalized structural models which in 1936 led Ralph Linton, in his *Study of Man*, to his famous formulation of the role-concept. Further important steps were the integration of the concept into more differentiated theoretical conceptions (Parsons, Nadel, Goffman)[1] and the first attempts to grasp social roles by the empirical methods of modern social research (Gross, Rommetveit, etc.).[2] In Germany the discussion was again taken up in 1958 in an essay that had the effect of a première: Ralf Dahrendorf's 'Homo Sociologicus, Ein Versuch zur Geschichte und Kritik der Kategorie der sozialen Rolle'. This essay is probably the most influential publication in theoretical sociology that has appeared in Germany since the war. Certainly it is the only one which has led to a many-sided public dispute.[3]

It is not immediately clear why there should be any special difficulties here. The circumstances, which the role-concept aims at showing, can be presented in a few sentences, together with a large part of the usual terminological differentiations. Within a specific culture all heads of family behave similarly; this is expected of them, and indeed to some extent demanded of them. We find further such similarities amongst all marriageable daughters, all medicine-men, all club officials. The role of the father is somehow related and attuned to other roles, e.g. of the mother and of the children (role-structures). But the particularly well co-ordinated role-structure of the domestic circle does not always prevent conflict between the various frames of reference of the father-role — father to mother, father to children

---

1   The listing of these three names is merely to draw attention to the variety in kind of the possible theoretical frames of reference. Compare Talcott Parsons, *The Social System* (London, 1952), especially pp. 25ff. ('parts' — 'status' — 'role'), pp. 39ff. ('institutions'), pp. 55ff. ('pattern-variables'); S. F. Nadel, *The Theory of Social Structures* (London, 1957 and 1962), for conceptual formulation, especially pp. 23ff. ('behaviour' — 'regard to others' — 'normative' — 'series of interconnected characteristics'); Erving Goffman, *The Presentation of Self in Everyday Life* (New York, 1959, 1st ed. 1956), especially for the two chapters on 'Performance' and 'Teams', pp. 17ff. and pp. 77ff.

2   N. C. Gross, W. S. Mason, A. W. McEachern, *Explorations in Role Analysis, Studies of the School Superintendency Role* (New York, 1958); Rangar R. Rommetveit, *Social Norms and Roles, Explorations in the Psychology of Enduring Social Pressures* (Oslo and Minneapolis, 1955).

3   In the meantime, Dahrendorf's essay has appeared in its 5th edition (Cologne and Opladen, 1965). Here, also, Dahrendorf's reply to numerous objections is printed again under the title 'Soziologie und menschliche Natur', which first appeared in 1963. For a discussion, compare above all Helmuth Plessner, 'Soziale Rolle und menschliche Natur', *Erkenntnis und Verantwortung. Festschrift für Theodor Litt* (Düsseldorf, 1960); Hans Paul Bahrdt, 'Zur Frage des Menschenbildes in der Soziologie', *Europäisches Archiv für Soziologie*, 1 (1961); Friedrich H. Tenbruck, 'Zur deutschen Rezeption der Rollenanalyse', *Kölner Zeitschrift für Soziologie*, 1 (1961); Judith Janoska-Bendl, 'Probleme der Freiheit in der Rollenanalyse', *Kölner Zeitschrift für Soziologie und Sozialpsychologie*, 3 (1962); Jürgen Habermas, *Theorie und Praxis* (Neuwied am Rhein und Berlin, 1963), pp. 173ff.; supplementarily, Dieter Claessens, 'Rolle und Verantwortung', *Soziale Welt*, 1 (1963).

(his role-sectors). Different demands are being made upon him from all sides — and moreover simultaneously (irreconcilable role-demands: intra-role-conflict). Often it is even more difficult to deal with the different demands of *different* social circles, the multitude of roles, or role-sets, which society imposes upon each individual as father, as lawyer and as club-chairman (inter-role-conflict). The individual would scarcely be able to support this burden if a structural relationship reaching beyond the different social circles did not provide for some compatibility; if, what is more, a system of role-allocation did not gradually prepare him (in a series of role-sequences) to assume a role, or else prevent him from, or hamper him in, combining roles which do not harmonize in this culture. That he becomes willing and able to submit to his role is taken care of by the process of socialization in which we learn to desire to do what we should and finally to do it without noticing it (inner social control, internalization of social roles). This process of learning incorporates future duties, e.g. when still a child we play at being a father and perhaps even a club official (anticipatory role-play). Should an unresolved remainder still be left over provision has been made that deviant conduct leads to unpleasant consequences (external control of role-behaviour, negative sanctions).

It is perhaps understandable that such a way of looking at things, if pursued consistently, provokes the question of how the irritating fact of society is in any way tolerable for the individual — or, conversely, the irritating fact of the individual for society. But such questions are at the same time misleading. They obviously impute a definite relationship between individual and role. The concept of social role, however, says nothing of how the individual is related to his role, of whether or how he reflects it. It denotes — at least this is the claim which Helmuth Plessner has so pertinently formulated — 'a structure in which every conception of the self can be realized', and thereby it ranks amongst those concepts of modern sociology which are formal enough to be 'variable when confronted with the social world in its ethnic and historical diversity without being tied to a specifically modern comprehension'.[1]

Here, however, it becomes clear why the case of employing this concept should be viewed with some reservation. What is really meant by this 'structure in which every conception of the self can be realized'? Is it merely a conceptual construction, or does this structure in fact exist, or does there exist 'something like' this structure? On what is the claim to *universal* applicability and variability based? Does this basic sociological concept express anything fundamental about the social existence of man, about the outlines of social relationships which must of necessity follow from the process of societation?

These are awkward questions. The discussion on the role-concept is determined less by these questions than by the answers implied. At the same time there is a tendency (not unjustified) towards alternately putting forward and then retracting

1   Helmuth Plessner, 'Soziale Rolle und menschliche Natur', p. 111 and p. 106.

answers which are methodologically dangerous. The 'peculiarly compelling quality'[1] of the role-concept provokes attempts at explanation which, however, run the risk of abandoning the sure rules of operational argument. Thereby arises an ambivalence to which, in my opinion, numerous uncertainties and controversies about the assumptions, formal conception and function of the concept can be traced back. The concept of social role is an analytical means of comprehending the coherence of social actions, and at the same time a means of construction for the representation of social structures. If one engages in questions which in some way or other go beyond this instrumental character of the concept — is there not then a danger that the previously mentioned erosion of the concept, the loss of detachment will be repeated on another level? That the concept will become a pattern of formulation for arbitrary statements about 'mere social existence'?

The following reflections are an attempt to show that the analytical and constructional function — which demand above all the greatest possible precision of the concept — may very well be combined with a 'fundamental' claim which can be given clear and verifiable formulation. These deliberations must, of course, be combined with the individual methodological steps in the abstraction of the concept. First it seems to me necessary to construct the premisses of the role-concept more clearly than has hitherto been the case.

II

The role-concept must not haul itself by its own boot-straps out of the morass of 'social phenomena' as if it were the beginning of all things in sociology. It is *deducible* from two more comprehensive concepts: *social normation* and *social differentiation,* or more exactly, from a certain linking of the two concepts.

Every society can be considered as a framework of behavioural normations. Certain regularities of action are constantly singled out as being obligatory and binding.

Every society can be considered as a socially differentiated structure, as a framework composed of socially dissimilar parts. Now there is naturally a continuum of social dissimilarities which permits an unlimited choice as to possibilities of classification. Let us restrict ourselves right now to those dissimilarities which are differences in the behaviour of certain classes of individuals. Such divergences may be found in all societies. They are always related to one another and thus can be seen as a structure.

Both statements are not only unusually obvious — they also belong amongst the

---

1   See Ralf Dahrendorf, 'Soziologie und menschliche Natur', p. 17. According to him, the concept of social role belongs to those categories which obtrude 'with a necessity which is difficult to explain' and 'although invented' appear 'not *merely* invented'. Similarly, F. H. Tenbruck, 'Zur deutschen Rezeption der Rollenanalyse', p. 2: in concepts like position, role, expectation and sanction 'general sociological understanding is invested'; they present to us 'the fundamentals of every society'.

most general statements that can be formulated with sociological concepts. If we ask for an explanation of the universality of social normation and social differentiation we have to bring in *expressis verbis* anthropological hypotheses.[1]

On the other hand the claim of universal applicability can also be upheld for particular *combinations* of the two concepts.

Starting from social differentiation we can say that by no means all behavioural differentiations tend to be binding, but that in every society some are normative. The structure of social dissimilarities constantly has a normative nucleus.

Starting from social normation we find that social norms are indeed valid for all members of a society ('of this fruit shall no man eat'), but in every society there exist norms which are only valid for certain classes of individuals. Social norms are of a nature which may be differentiated. If one sees the norms of various levels of differentiation of a certain society in their context then one can speak of a 'pigeon-holing' and specialization, of a *compartmentalizing of norms*. To give us a rough overall view we shall make use of the image of the tree whose trunk (the general norms, which are valid for all members of the society) spreads out into branches (the norms of membership of special social units, e.g. of all members of families, of all employees of companies) and finally divides into twigs (norms of fathers in contrast to norms of mothers, or of foremen as opposed to those of workers).

Now, the differentiation of norms frequently continues beyond the stage of the twigs. They follow extremely peripheral social differentiations and sometimes can even be found in very shortlived groupings. If we do not wish to include the infinitely large sphere in which social differentiation and normation intermingle, it is expedient to delimit the concept of social differentiation more sharply than we have done till now. The relatively best starting-point is probably offered by certain phenomena of differentiation which may be termed *positional crystallization*.

In a first approach these positional crystallizations may be characterized as a 'cluster' made up of a whole series of social behavioural peculiarities which are associated with a certain class of individuals; further, these 'clusters' are relatively long-lived and can, for example, be transmitted from one generation to another. Since individual examples of such 'clusters' are related to others, there can arise, in the case of a delay in transmission – and this is probably the clearest phenomenon – the feeling of a vacancy (the missing father, the missing priest, the missing foreman). This feeling of a vacancy shows that here are certain places 'reserved' in the framework of social differentiations, something that ought to be 'filled'. Thus

---

1   It is worth considering the possible lines of deduction and the necessary premises of such explanations. The deduction of social norms in this sense appears to me quite plainly constructable. Very much more difficult is the deduction of social differentiation, even when the concept is considerably more narrowly defined, e.g. in the sense of positional differentiations (see below). Moreover, this is one of the (by no means numerous) sociological problems which might be pursued quite meaningfully through the individual historical stages of the 'invention' of sociology.

social differentiation here is not linked to the fact that certain individuals have certain qualities or abilities which are then combined with certain behaviour expectations. Just the reverse: certain clusters of behaviour-expectations are fixed and await individuals whose characteristics and qualities appear suited for the allocation of these behaviour-clusters. Many social activities have the purpose of ensuring that this waiting is not in vain. The process of allocation is organized in every society according to definite principles and methods. This too underlines the stable, fixed character of these places, their 'positional' level.

Only where such positional crystallization is demonstrable — where social differentiation has attained this distinct profile — shall we ask further questions as to which of the expected behavioural peculiarities have normative character. (We can assume that in positional crystallization *always some* behavioural peculiarities are socially binding.) These modes of behaviour that are expected as being obligatory we term role-norms. Social roles accordingly are clusters of role-norms, specialized normative sub-systems which are related to one another.

Just as the concept of position delimits the sphere of role-analysis so it also shows the interval, the distance which separates role-phenomena from the particular case, the individual. For the occupants of social positions the normative sub-systems are laid down in advance — as duties and rights. Thus it is misleading to call social role an 'elementary concept which does justice to the individual also, or rather, to the fact that individuals exist'.[1] How far roles may be individualized, or rather, how far the individual may succeed in individualization of his behaviour is a question all on its own. But it must be noted that social roles are of a collective nature, a ready-to-wear social garment. They make *like* demands on the *different* occupants of like positions. Social roles, seen from the point of view of society, are indeed phenomena of normative specialization; seen from the standpoint of the individual they are phenomena of social generalization.

III

Let us at once examine the dividing lines that result from this deduction. This is best done by means of a comparison with similar neighbouring phenomena which, by the distinctions we have drawn, we have sectioned off from the concept of role. At the same time we must ask how these phenomena can be related to the concept.

We may begin with the great example of charismatic rule. The charismatic leader in Max Weber's sense establishes without doubt a normative differentiation of a new kind. The appropriate behaviour-patterns can indeed be borrowed from tradition, they can imitate certain archetypes of the prophet, of the deliverer in time of distress, of the inspired envoy. In reviving and modifying such archetypes, however, and above all in finally asserting them in the face of the accepted structures, the charismatic leader creates normative situations *sui generis.* Yet we would not

1   Hans Paul Bahrdt, 'Zur Frage des Menschenbildes in der Soziologie', p. 6.

immediately speak of the 'role' of the charismatic leader here, nor of a 'role-structure' of his immediate circle. The positional crystallization is lacking. Only when the process of 'becoming commonplace' ('Veralltäglichung') is accomplished does positional crystallization build up. It manifests itself — this is, by the way, the essential stand-point of Max Weber — in the successful resolution of the problem of a successor. In this process it is not of course the act of passing on, the transference of leadership to another person, that is decisive. Rather the decisive question is whether the charismatic pattern of the leader's behaviour can be so re-formed — rendered so commonplace — that it becomes at all transmissible. We can also say, the decisive fact is whether a position can develop whose rights and duties can be exercised not just by one individual in his uniqueness. Only with the de-individual-ization of norms are role-norms formed. (And correspondingly we would say only with the consolidation of charismatic power to positional power does 'Herrschaft' come about.)

But let us take other, more banal cases. With *social behavioural types* such as, for example, the snob, the dandy, the beatnik and the bohemian, not only positional character is lacking but also a normative behavioural differentiation. Within their own specific milieu there can indeed arise constellations in which the representation of such behaviour-types is demanded, in which a certain class of people are committed to them. But here it is a case of general normative expectations of membership. Typically any further differentiation within the general conditions of belonging is absent. Outside their specific milieu these obligations too dissolve: the social behaviour type is, as a character-mask, to be assumed arbitrarily, at the disposal of everyone. We are also free to select and borrow only some of the stylistic elements, to create new combinations with them and to bring them 'on stage' while still keeping within the limits of our roles at that moment.[1] Certain social behaviour types can even be predestined to combine with certain social roles, such as, for example, the *jeune ingenu* or the *enfant terrible* with the role of the better-class daughter. But here also things go no further than the supply of patterns for the supplementary standardization of behaviour, no further than the exploitation of rights of privilege.

Closer still to the phenomenon of role are figures which I should like to call *group-figures.* As a rule they develop within more enduring informal groups, as youth groups perhaps, and have then the character of surrogates of social roles. They can, however, also arise within role-structures — in an office perhaps — as additional models of expected behaviour. Such group-figures are, for example, the man of initiative and the producer of ideas whose brainwaves are awaited by all, the fool and the 'talker', the confidant and the father-confessor, the diplomatic type who takes care of the external relations of the group — and finally, of course, the

---

1   Helmuth Plessner, 'Soziale Rolle und menschliche Natur', p. 107 (role as a 'social functional element of society' and as a performance expectation, and not as an 'arbitrary behavioural cloak').

highly varying types of leader and so-called 'nobody' or whipping-boy. The appropriate behaviour-expectations concentrate, in the course of the process of societation, on certain persons. Desirable functions are shared out. While all this is happening the interplay between all the parts can enter into such accord that the distribution of group figures clicks naturally into place: interplay seems to be dependent upon a certain person playing the group-figure, or even monopolizing it for himself. Since each person has himself repeatedly played a part in bringing about the development of such group-structures, and will also continue to play such a part, there is a relatively large store of general experience here. Thus each is aware that it can be difficult to break free again from such models of expected behaviour. And also a certain illusion will often repeat itself: at times it seems as if the group-figures were tailored to the individuality of the participants, indeed as if they were invented for the respective individuals. Yet a comparison easily shows that even these group-figures already lie ready and waiting as standardized behaviour-patterns. In the most diverse groups they are reproduced in very similar form, or are even directly imitated. The basic outline may in a certain culture vary but little from the kindergarten to adult circles, to the old people's home.

But however forcefully these group-figures might occasionally impress themselves on the individual, for the function of roles they lack, as a rule, any normative weight. The general norms of membership of such groups, such as solidarity without and camaraderie and fairness within, are not specialized any further. The individual group-figures do indeed belong to the model of expected behaviour but are not burdened with any obligation. The explanation for this lies close at hand. These often easily-terminable groupings might for the most part not be equal to the burden of a *differentiated* normative structure. They can only bear limited normative demands. The demands must concentrate on and restrict themselves to the exigencies of general cohesion, the minimum of general membership norms.

Certainly, groups may also be observed which develop further and which are successful in the normation of group-figures. In such cases the decisive factor must always be a process of increasing hierarchization. Such a process can finally reach a stage at which the leaders are able to demand and to establish differentiated behaviour norms. Then there arise the first shadows of social roles, quasi-roles. Only when positional crystallization is successful, that is, when the group-figures detach themselves as normative sub-systems and become independent from the individuals involved, should we speak of the genesis of new role-structures. Here this example resembles the first, the transformation of charismatic power into positional role.

Group-figures, just like social behaviour types, are prototypes for the standardization of behaviour. When, for example, we want to overcome an uncertainty in our behaviour we feel these prototypes to be quite practical. We can stylize our attitudes without first having to invent the style, and without running the risk that this might not be generally understood. To these prototypes there belongs a further group which we shall call *individuality patterns.* These individuality patterns have the property of offering blueprints which seem to hint at something quite individual – they give directions as to how one should play the individual. The tough, grumbling, brusque, blustering superior with the heart of gold who does not really mean any harm – the vulgar businessman with the sentimental ways – the elegant, elderly lady with her shocking free-and-easy heartiness – can be thoroughly socially standardized modes of behaviour, but they are, as it happens, also standardized forms of putting oneself across as an *individual.* The typical, pre-fabricated quality of these individuality-patterns is glossed over by the fact that they appear to contain inner contradictions, that they unite the (apparently) incompatible, and as it were emphasize a calculated inconsistency. But in this very contradictoriness, in this surprise effect, lies their suitability for use in playing the individual. And on the same basis we are concerned here with 'nameless types', with types which we cannot name with one word: if this were possible their typological character would lie exposed to view, and playing the individual (insofar as it lays store by itself) would have to move off into less articulated realms. Obviously, these patterns are conditioned by culture and social level to a large extent. Over and above this they are especially closely linked with certain social roles (e.g. with the role of the superior) – a supply of further ways of moulding behaviour which society puts on the market as a 'free gift' together with certain role-duties.

The significance of this phenomenon – familiar to us today, perhaps, from advertisements or so-called 'human-interest' literature – presupposes not only the presence of the individualist notion in our history of ideas, but also the dissemination of the representation of individuality as a social model of expected behaviour throughout a whole society. It presupposes that without individuality one is no longer acceptable. But this being the case it must also be shown how it is achieved.

This enumeration of a few examples at once makes clear certain dividing-lines. The first example (the charismatic leader) shows that we should not term any behavioural pattern which remains tied to the never-to-be-repeated uniqueness of a certain person as social role. Positional crystallization is lacking here. The three subsequent examples (social behaviour-types, group-figures, individuality-patterns) demonstrate that we should not term all behaviour-patterns which have the function of social differentiation as social roles. As a rule even the normative content is lacking here.

These last three examples give, however, a further indication. In all three cases *just as with the role-phenomenon,* we are dealing with creations in which we participate occasionally more or less actively, but which usually tend to achieve their own independence and confront us as 'givens'. In taking over these set forms of behaviour we represent something that is more and perhaps also less than we ourselves, but in any case something which is *not congruent* with the individual as something individual. The congruence does not presuppose an especially advanced process of individuation; it is sufficient to accept that even people who have assumed and assimilated exactly the same behaviour-patterns still differ from one another: that perfect congruence of social behavioural standardizations with the complexity of individual physical make-up and temperaments, experiences and vagaries, preferences, anxieties and passions, is unattainable. This, however, is also to say that a 'structure making possible every conception of the self' comprising social 'givens' and individuals (i.e. the incongruence of standard and individual case) is always to be found. And therewith remains *in principle* the possibility that the individual reflects the standardizations of the behaviour which he has taken over as a 'being for others', as merely represented individuality, as a double image of himself.[1] Now, our examples show that this structure by no means characterizes only 'the basic relationship of social role and human nature'.[2] The structure of the double image goes deeper. It repeats itself at the most diverse levels of social standardization.

Accordingly it appears that 'the individual and society are mediated' by no means only in the concept of social role.[3] All behaviour-patterns are aimed at such mediatorial functions. What we are singling out from amongst these mediatorial functions − and correspondingly from amongst these double-image structures − as 'social role' is only a limited range of phenomena.

IV

The deduction of the role-concept was attempted with a twofold intention: firstly, the relationship with other fundamental sociological concepts was to be made clear right from the start; but above all, the premises which go into constructing the concept had to be clarified. The comparison with neighbouring phenomena showed some dividing lines which arise out of this attempt. We also saw, however, that the doubling and incongruence of behaviour-pattern and individual person is not a peculiarity of role-norms, but is necessarily a connotation of every social behavioural standardization. A similar deliberation will now be repeated on a different level. In this we shall refer to phenomena of societation which we have hitherto imputed.

All the behaviour-patterns discussed, including social roles, are conglomerates of several actions. Ordinarily we see these individual actions as a meaningful unit − the role of the father, the style of the dandy, the conduct of the eccentric − i.e. we do

1 Helmuth Plessner, 'Soziale Rolle und menschliche Natur', pp. 111ff.
2 *Ibid.* p. 115. In Plessner's article it says − though with a different aim in view − that man 'only arrives at his own nature by virtue of the doubling in a role-figure with which he attempts to identify himself. This potential identification of every person with something which he is not of himself proves to be the only constant in the basic relationship of social roles and human nature'.
3 Ralf Dahrendorf, 'Soziologie und menschliche Natur', p. 15. The same idea occurs quite frequently. Moreover, I do not believe that the superiority of the conceptual starting-point 'role', as compared with 'social actions' and 'social relation', can be argued with regard to such mediatorial functions.

not expressly reflect upon the fact that in situation 'a' we expect from the bearer of
the father-role action 'b' (or, negatively, in any case *not* action 'c'), and that our
image of the role is composed of a sum-total of such expected individual actions.
If we now look more closely at these individual actions, the simplest and apparently
most banal thing that may be said about them is that, in like situations they *repeat*
themselves in like form. In other words, social behaviour-patterns are composed of
uniformities in behaviour.

Expectation of, and preparedness for, such behavioural uniformities would,
however, be unthinkable without an agreement by society on a series of *processes
of abstraction.* We can clarify this by one simple example. When we enter a shop in
order to buy tobacco there follows a certain interaction, which repeats itself a
hundredfold, between purchasers acting according to a social stereotype and sales-
assistants also acting to a social stereotype. More strictly speaking, however, both
parties act differently every time. So in actual fact the uniformity which is all-
important here lies somewhere in the middle between 'identical' and 'different'.
The possible discrepancy is limited; if the limit is overstepped the purchase will not
go through. But the requisite uniformity in behaviour is likewise limited: if it had
to attain the degree of uniformity of a military drill in order that the purchase
could go through, many people would probably prefer to give up smoking. What
(still) counts as uniform and what does not (any longer) rests therefore upon a
social arrangement. And this social arrangement refers to certain selected
characteristics which are abstracted from these courses of action which are
actually taking place.

Uniform modes of behaviour, behavioural regularities in this sense are thus not
an invention of sociology, but are an invention of society.[1] It could now be shown
why the construction of such behavioural stereotypes must be accomplished in
every closer-knit and more enduring societation. But let us restrict ourselves here to
the process of abstraction itself.

Simple behavioural regularities, in the sense of that which is merely current, of
expected social usage or 'common practice', are already the product of such
abstractions. But even here a basic phenomenon of societation does not stand out
more clearly until behaviour-norms are established: namely as the *demand* that the

---

1 If we maintain that in a certain situation persons of category A (cyclists) repeatedly act in a
uniform way, the judgement of 'uniformity' might in the first instance be determined by
arbitrarily fixed criteria of the observer. If, on the other hand, it can be shown that other
persons, say persons of category B (pedestrians), regulate their actions from the outset by
certain expected uniform behaviour from A, then we are inferring this 'uniformity' from
relationship of actions, a pattern of interaction. What behaviour B expects, presupposes and
imputes of A — what may still be counted as 'uniform' and what no longer may — we can
infer from the behaviour of the B-persons, their 'anticipated reaction'. At the same time we
must as a rule impute no more than that B, for example, wants only to avoid a collision (or
effect a purchase). The relationship of behavioural regularity, orientation, and predictability,
which is only roughly indicated here, is to be presented in detail at another point. In my
opinion it is also worth explaining why we are seldom conscious of carrying out processes.

process of abstraction be fulfilled. This is even more the case with the tendency to ascribe moral value to the pure correctness of the completed abstraction. This is just as valid for the course of action as it is for the recognition of normatively relevant situations. ('*Now* this norm is valid' — 'When you pass through *this* door' — 'At *this* cross-road'.) Tolerance towards deviating individual situational experiences in which the characteristics appropriate to the norm are not recognized, is constantly limited and must be limited. In the case of *role-norms* the demand for abstraction refers now not just to situation and course of action but, in addition, also to the persons participating at this moment. We can only act in conformity with our roles if we can give ourselves and those concerned at that moment the correct social classification, if we can recognize therefore the particular social position to which they are bound. Strange to say we almost always manage this. We are in a position to see ourselves and other people actually *as* a businessman, *as* a student, *as* colleagues and *as* fathers. That we can see ourselves and others in this way and that we can transpose this perception into behavioural orientation is a condition for acting in accordance with our role.

Whatever tricks, therefore, sociology might perform in forming the role-concept (as in forming other fundamental concepts) a trick of society underlies them: i.e. underlying the sociological abstraction is a social abstraction. One can describe role-phenomena without starting out from sharply delimited sociological abstractions. But one cannot describe them without keeping the fact in view that these phenomena themselves represent abstractions, and what is more, abstractions which those engaged in social action carry out and must carry out. They come about only because we, in forming ourselves into societies, *conceive of action taking place on abstractive levels of reality.*

All behavioural standardizations are, in this sense, a chain of 'constructive' actions and interactions, extremely artificial phenomena out of which, in a process of secondary, once more 'superimposed' abstraction, we attempt to delimit the role phenomena — at the point of intersection of social normation and positional differentiation.

V

Now obviously, for the formation of a concept, specific *sociological abstractions* are necessary which separate out further characteristics from the context described. The analytical usefulness of the concept is by no means already proven when, in a description, we can, with the aid of selected examples, draw a few dividing-lines. We must formulate criteria which can be illustrated not just by means of 'case-studies' but which may also be found in unprepared empirical material.

Here, the heavy emphasis on the *normative* significance of social role, which the deduction of the concept already attempted to show, seems to me to be of

---

1   Compare below, the deliberations of Georg Simmel on the 'theory of cognition of society', Section VI, pp. 30-34.

particular value. If we stick consistently to this criterion the result is — in comparison with the definitions of the role so far offered — a particularly restrictively-constructed concept. At the same time we do not abandon the common basis of the discussion so far. The normative content of social roles is being imputed almost continuously, and most of the time is even expressly made prominent. The proposal that we stick more exactly to this hard core of the role-concept has in my opinion, first and foremost, the advantage that it increases the *aptitude for discrimination* of the concept and therewith also the comparableness of the results of research. At the same time it has the result that we do not just add here some further variant to a hotch-potch of suggestions for a definition. On the contrary, the proposal is suited to making clear the relationship of the variants so far offered. It is exactly this comparatively narrowly-defined criterion which shows what possibilities for extending the analysis present themselves under certain conditions.

In the first case, our formulation of the concept unites merely the two components of social normation and social (positional) differentiation. We denote as social role a cluster of *behaviour norms* which a certain category of members of a society, or else of a group, has, *in contradistinction* to others, to fulfil. Further delimiting definitions can now be obtained by increasing the preciseness of the concept of behaviour norms — and more especially, of the role-norm. To do this a series of distinctions is necessary and I shall set them down here one after the other, in the form of a list.[1] These distinctions are not determined by the attempt to 'cover' as large a part as possible of social reality conceptually, or to grasp as thoroughly as possible all essential factors. On the contrary, we shall follow Durkheim's rule of maintaining the greatest possible 'externality' in sociological conceptual criteria, i.e. we shall refer only to facts which stand out clearly, and on which as much as possible depends.

1. We term as behaviour norms modes of behaviour which, in a certain situation, are repeated uniformly by all, or by a certain category, of the members of a society or group, and which, in the case of deviation, are asserted by means of negative sanctions against persons deviating. We shall refer, therefore, to *behaviour which actually goes on,* and not to behaviour which is wished-for, or thought to be obligatory, or which is subjectively expected.

We term as behaviour both actions in the narrow sense of the word (including any discernable abstention, but also including a person's dress for example) and also

---

1 In what follows numerous judgements are made which ought to be substantiated in more detail. Here, however, a comprehensive summary may suffice, partly following up my essay, 'Soziale Normen', *Europäisches Archiv für Soziologie,* 27 (1961), 185ff. Gerd Spittler has put forward an empirical investigation, which starts out from the point of view evolved here, and develops attempts at explaining certain sanctioning actions, in his Freiburg dissertation, 'Norm und Sanktion, Untersuchungen zum Sanktionsmechanismus'. This work is based on participant observation in the activities of a luxury restaurant-kitchen and of a private clinic. It appeared in 1967, in the series Texte und Dokumente zur Soziologie (Walter-Verlag, Olten und Freiburg im Breisgau).

linguistic manifestations. Here again it is frequently expedient to distinguish between linguistic form of expression (like choice of words, use of standardized formulations, slang, etc.) and speech-content, or meaning. All the behavioural modes mentioned can receive normative character: abstention as a normative prohibition, tabooed action; dress generally in the sense of 'decency', and especially in the sense of certain role-attributes, e.g. of a judge, of a soldier (action-norms); linguistic form-of-expression in the sense of reproduction of certain stereotypes in the 'correct' situations, but also as the commitment to jargon, dialect etc. (verbal-norms); expressed opinion — with or without being tied to fixed linguistic formulae — as a duty to demonstrate one's opinion, explicit assent or disapproval (opinion-norms).[1]

Correspondingly, the concepts which denote the relational structures of social roles should also be orientated not towards expectations but towards behavioural criteria: 'norm-recipient' — 'norm-beneficiary' — 'disposer of sanctions' — 'norm-sender'. Every role-player is a *norm-recipient* in so far as he is tied to modes of behaviour from which he may not deviate without consequence. He is a *norm-beneficiary* in so far as others in relation to him are tied to sanctioned modes of behaviour. The passive component of his role, a stock of rights in relation to others, is recognizable, among other things, by the fact that in the case of infringements a direct right of sanction is granted to him, or by the fact that he can come forward as a plaintiff, that restitution may be made to him etc. (Every behaviour norm is obviously related to recipients, but not every behaviour norm — and also not every role-norm — is directed towards a definite member of a society as beneficiary.) *Disposers of sanctions* are the organs of decisions about sanctions and the organs of their execution. Their specific distribution and the extent of their rights is probably the characteristic of role-structures which is most rich in consequences. *Norm-senders,* we call those members of a society within the sphere of validity of a norm who, by assent or disapprobation, by demonstrative readiness for action or positive intervention, protect the validity of the norm.

In this way the basic concepts are not related to behavioural orientations, nor to

---

1   On the normative level the distinction between speech contents and actions receives a special stress. It is not just to reinforce the everyday experience that frequently people do not do what they say, and do not say what they do. We may not even impute at all that certain normative speech contents are also normative as action-contents. Between opinion- and action-norms of a society there can exist a continual 'constructional' discrepancy. There is no lack of examples in our society. Obviously one can take them as proofs of the subjectively dual morality of individuals. But at the same time, the discrepancy between opinion- and action-norms can also be understood as a possible constructional principle of social norm-structures, which, in certain circumstances, contributes towards raising the degree of norm-conformity on *both* levels. Opinion norms can (e.g. in the case of sexual demands) form an advanced protective ring which secures a normative nucleus in actions. The identity of the two as to content would here call both in question. In such cases the normative nucleus of the actions does not draw life from an individual, dual morality, but from a social system of double consciousness.

behaviour-expectations; they do not pre-suppose appropriate assumptions, but they always remain open to supplementations of this sort. Thus we do not impute, for example, that a norm-recipient really orientates himself by the demands and expectations of his beneficiary. Quite apart from the case of lasting internalization the norm-recipient can, if occasion should arise, also act in accordance with his role when orientating himself by alien groups, imaginary heroes, and archetypes of every kind that have nothing directly to do with the structure of recipient − beneficiary − disposer of sanctions − norm-sender. The beneficiary is in this case the person of reference of his behaviour, but not − in Robert Merton's sense − the person of reference for his behavioural orientation.[1] Nor do we impute that a putting-into-effect of sanctions is preceded by an expectation as to what the other 'should have done'. Sometimes only deviation from customary regularity of behaviour can eventually lead to the 'revelation' that a normative interpretation is appropriate here.

This passes over in silence the fact that the occupants of interrelated positions tend to be linked by behaviour-expectations and behavioural demands. But how the subjective horizon of expectation, how the frame of reference of orientation appears at any one moment we often cannot discern with any certainty from the behaviour sequence. It is also at least misleading when in many definitions of role, concepts like behaviour, expectation, demand and orientation are short-circuited.

After what has been said the methodological priorities of role-analysis are obvious. The primary approach towards identifying actions and action-norms is visual observation, watching. Reports, conversations and interrogations can (so long as they aim at concrete information about who, in a certain situation, did this or that) serve as a secondary source. The primary approach towards identifying linguistic behaviour and behaviour-norms in speech is listening, either when listening as a third party or when taking part in conversation. Now, it is of course clear that empirical social research mostly does not, and cannot keep to these priorities. The interrogative method is so practicable and elastic that it can almost always be steered, by some round-about way, 'into the vicinity' of the problem posed. Thus this method is also well to the fore in the empirical research that has been done so far. At the same time, the abiding confidence that asking questions always produces some results, is confirmed. But here too some clarifications and terminological distinctions are expedient.

To attempt to ascertain linguistic behaviour-norms by asking questions is

---

1   It might be expedient that the concepts of reference-group and reference-individual in Merton's sense (that is, as groups or persons by which someone orientates himself normatively, or else, by comparison) be retained. As well as Merton's essays (in *Social Theory and Social Structure* (Glencoe, Ill., 1957), also clarifying in our context are W. Contu, 'Role-playing versus role-taking, an appeal for clarification', *American Sociological Review,* 16 (1951), 180ff., and R. H. Turner, 'Role taking, role standpoint and reference group behavior', *American Journal of Sociology,* 61 (1956), 316ff.

B

difficult; the reaction to deviating behaviour can really only be reliably established in group conversations. Drawing conclusions about valid norms of actions from reports about certain action-sequences is likewise a questionable and laborious process. Purely documentary reports in any case gain weight as evidence if they are supplemented by observational methods. On the other hand, one frequently meets with the type of question-asking which prompts the persons being questioned to make generalizing judgements: e.g. about frequent 'typical' actions, about 'what is generally expected', about 'right' and 'wrong' actions and moral demands or desires and ideals. In the broadest framework of role-analysis the result here is that in principle there are three possibilities of interpretation.

In the first case statements of this kind can be deemed indications of actual behaviour-sequences and also especially of behaviour-norms. The conclusiveness of this procedure is a question of the interpretative skill of the authors and the inclination of the reader. Further to this, attempts can be made to draw conclusions as to the subjective expectation-horizon of the person questioned, his orientation, needs and values, which accompany and direct his behaviour. The results may, for example, be assembled into *'role-images'*, or rather, *'ideal-role-images'* of the persons questioned. Taking this a step further, the image held by the occupants of certain social roles, the image held by outsiders and the image which the occupants imagine to be the image held by outsiders, can all be related to one another.[1] The aim here, as a rule, is to ascertain the degree of consensus and to obtain clues for the degree of legitimacy of prevailing norms. To me the interpretative value of these results appears to be heavily dependent on whether the actual validity of the norm is known independently of the interpreted statements.

Finally, an interpretation is possible which foregoes breaking into the plane of verbalized opinion in any way. It takes the statements at their word, as a reality *sui generis,* without wishing to detach the influence of various degrees of reflection, the influence of linguistic facility, of opinion-norms etc. Research reports which base themselves thus on the intrinsic value of verbalized reality are methodologically particularly unproblematic. It is obviously possible at this level to assemble (verbal) role-images and ideal-role-images. The privileged position of the interrogative method and preference for a method which is foolproof can admittedly lead empirical sociology to develop into an encyclopaedic collection of facts about unrelated linguistic behaviour.

2. The development of behaviour-norms presupposes that *behavioural regularities* can be observed. (Mere obedience from case to case without constitution of behavioural regularities still does not establish behaviour-norms even when it is a matter of sanctioned behaviour.) Regularity in behaviour may not be measured in isolation by the mere frequency of certain behaviour-sequences ('the Japanese tend to bow frequently'). Situational characteristics must constantly be included as

---

1   Compare especially R. Rommetveit, *Social Norms and Roles,* pp. 123ff.

initial conditions which mostly or frequently lead to certain behaviour-sequences.[1] The inclusion of the situation and the processes of abstraction out of which 'like situations' and 'like behaviour-sequences' result are, as has already been shown, effects of the process of societation itself. We must not invent, but find, these similarities.

However, sociological representation of behavioural regularities will, as a rule, work with considerable simplifications. A limited number of observations tends to be more or less quickly reduced to principles and to be compounded into mostly very general 'normative statements' which are approximated to the language and way of thinking of our legal codifications. This results in numerous difficulties, especially in cultural comparison.[2]

Quantification of frequencies also presents further problems (even when the situation-behaviour model is heavily simplified). It is usual and also often sufficient to circumscribe frequencies in a rather non-committal way with indefinite numbers. Comparative formulations like, 'in situation S behaviour A is more frequent than behaviour B', or more exactly, 'A is more frequent than non-A', go one step further. Now, quantifications of the greatest possible exactitude are, however, often desirable, e.g. in analysing changes in norms. To this end the model of the validity-structure of norms can be strongly differentiated, but it must at least contain the distinction between (a) cases of behaviour-validity (conformity), (b) cases of sanction-validity (deviation but sanctioned), and (c) cases of invalidity (deviation, not sanctioned).[3] According to our definition only modes of behaviour in which some a-cases and at least one b-case can be verified, are *identifiable* as normative.[4] On the other hand we do not assume that norms have a comparatively high behavioural regularity.

---

1 Certain behaviour norms, however, are to be characterized by means of their relatively high detachment from situation – though one should not let oneself be deceived here by the corresponding norm-statements. The norm-statement 'Thou shalt not kill', in our culture, for example, by no means denotes a norm detached from situation.

2 Compare the characterization of the norm-structure of primitive cultures by the formulation of 'underlying postulates' in Adamson Hoebel's, *The Law of Primitive Man. A Study in Comparative Legal Dynamics* (Cambridge, Mass., 1954), pp. 69f., 104f., 131, 142f., 191f., 252ff. Certainly Hoebel is aware of the problem. He demands an improvement of the empirical investigation as an essential condition of the further development of the formation of theory in the ethnology of law.

3 This is in the sense of Theodor Geiger's *Vorstudien zu einer Soziologie des Rechts* (Neuwied am Rhein und Berlin, 1964, 1st ed. 1947). But Geiger does not put his finger expressly on the distinction between 'behaviour-validity' and 'sanction-validity', and this leads to some obscurities.

4 Here the question of identifiability must be strictly separated from suppositions about actual validity of a norm. Compare also, Geiger's statements on the 'doubt-formula' (the non-verifiability of b-cases), *Vorstudien zu einer Soziologie des Rechts,* pp. 96ff. A similar doubt-formula can be formulated in the event of non-verifiability of a-cases. Here, as always, ascertainments can be compensated by reasoned assumptions. Only, it must remain clear whether these assumptions are related to the characterization of behaviour as normative, or to a certain validity-structure of the behaviour norm.

3. We distinguish behaviour-norms from other social regularities by a rather palpable characteristic, e.g. *negative sanctions in reaction* to deviating behaviour. This obviously does not mean that we see in negative sanction the 'origin' of an obligation. No more is it assumed that the behavioural validity of social norms is to be traced back solely or in essentials to methods of external social control. The definition does not limit the significance of the processes of socialization and of role-internalization for role-analysis. Tenbruck rightly reminds us that 'when all aspects of a role are rigorously pursued, the investigation must inevitably extend over the whole structure and culture of society'.[1] However we are not concerned here with the question of where to stop, but of where and how to start.[2]

Negative sanctions can have a content clearly delimitable as a behavioural action: censure, atonement, banishment, etc. ('specific sanctions'). They can, however, also spread over social relations as 'non-specific sanctions'. The person who deviates is avoided relatively frequently, he is less often taken into confidence, his word no longer counts for anything, and so on. Such a withdrawal of the usual 'benefits of societation' is often a more developed form of specific sanctions. But possibly it is the only observable reaction. In order to avoid becoming vague at this point we shall only count such reactions as sanctions (specific or unspecific) when they are directed against the person deviating, with the intention of being *recognizable as a reply* to certain behaviour.[3] (Thus, for example, not gossip behind a person's back, or reprisals which, in a confrontation with the person affected, are masked as 'coincidence'.) This distinction should, as a rule, be sufficient. Its justification lies in the fact that only a reaction which is intended to be recognizable to the person concerned as a reply to his deviant behaviour declares itself *for* the validity of the infringed norm. Only a reaction of this kind not only affects the person of the deviant, but is also at the same time an affirmation of the infringed norm.

In principle there would be no objection to including positive sanctions here too. But difficulties present themselves which are evidently frequently overlooked.[4]

---

1   F. H. Tenbruck, 'Zur deutschen Rezeption der Rollenanalyse', p. 25. His case of the traffic policeman is a good practice example.

2   If this is agreed upon, one should not play down, on the other hand, the factors of external pressure and compulsion. There are for instance, in my opinion, no reasons to deplore the fact that sociological analysis tends towards giving the picture 'of a tremendous pressure'. 'That is true of no culture' (A. M. Rose, *Sociology* (New York, 1956), p. 71 and p. 84, quotes from Tenbruck, 'Zur deutschen Rezeption der Rollenanalyse', p. 5 and p. 11). Such friendly claims can really only be made sociologically relevant if one, in addition, looks up on the map where the author lives (and simultaneously looks at the time).

3   This according to a suggestion by Gerd Spittler; compare note 1 on p. 23 above.

4   In my opinion numerous obscurities follow here from neglect of the analysis of sanction-actions. Correspondingly, customary classifications are also in need of revision, especially also the much-quoted proposals of Radcliffe-Brown, *Social Sanctions, Structure and Function in Primitive Society* (2nd ed., London, 1956), and R. Maunier, *Precis d'un traité de sociologie* (Paris, 1943). If it were still realizable I would suggest giving up totally the designations 'positive' and 'negative' sanctions. They simulate a parallelism of the phenomena and functions, which may not be imputed *en bloc*.

Some indications will have to suffice. As a result of a certain action which conforms to the norm, what commonly happens is — nothing. In any event, nothing special which would stand out from the usual process of interaction. (Exceptions are primarily rewards for conformity as aids to the learning-process in education.) Non-specific positive sanctions — especially trust, respect, and high 'contact-value' — are seldom associated with single actions, but rather draw up a 'behavioural balance'. But where unequivocally specific positive sanctions can be ascertained there follows a further difficulty in allocation: they are often related to standards of behaviour which are *not identical* with behaviour-norms. (The mere relationship of sense-contents is of no help to us here.) At the root of proposals to include positive sanctions in the analysis of social norms there seems, on the other hand, to lie the idea that positive and negative sanctions can be arranged in the sense of a scale in which the behaviour-norms function as the zero. Such continuous scales, however, can only be constructed if, from the start, one conceives of behavioural standardizations as a continuum of achievements, and in doing so, sacrifices the relatively clear definition of norms. If one adheres to this definition, then the analysis of positively sanctioned standards of behaviour must be separated off as a special, supplementary task. This task might be characterized as an inquiry into the areas of norm-free behaviour with reference to *specific opportunities* which certain social roles offer.

4. The concept of role should characterize the special *normative situation of the occupants of certain positions.* This does not mean that analysis must restrict itself to role-norms. Accepted behavioural regularities, social customs can likewise be included. I just suggest that the dividing-line be drawn as clearly as possible, and that terminological distinction be made between *role-norm* and *role-customs.* The identification of role-norms has to precede every supplementary reference to role-customs. Analysis of such role-customs — just like the analysis of the specific standards connected with positive sanctions — would, in the inquiry, have to be counted in the area of norm-free behaviour. One must not, therefore, imagine this norm-free area as a socially unformed sphere; for its part, it is stamped by social standardizations in many ways.

The fact that empirical separation of norm and custom is not always easy and often requires very close examination rests, among other things, on the fact that customs are often settled in the vicinity of social norms, and function as a sort of early-warning system. Accordingly, the fact that a person conforms to customs awakens confidence that he will conform to norms; deviation from customs arouses mistrust.[1] (Whoever does not act in conformity with customs 'is not too particular in any other sphere either'.) This connection, moreover, also explains the over-emphasized conformity to customs of social climbers, as of newcomers in general.

We have already hinted at a further distinction at an earlier point. The normative

---

1   The function of many social customs is similar in this respect to that of opinion-norms. Compare note 1 on p. 24.

situation of a role is characterized by the specific norms of a particular position; but for the normative situation of the occupant of the position and 'role-player' the *general norms,* which are valid for all members of a society are also relevant, and the *norms of membership* which apply to all members of an intermediate unit. This distinction is not so artificial that we, as socially active persons (as an accountant, as a husband), do not also frequently reflect it, e.g. when our particular duties and rights clash with those in general. How exactly we must, at any one time, make this distinction when analysing role-structures is, however, another question. It should be self-evident that it must not be worked to death as an end in itself. As indeed in general the demands for exactitude that have been developed here should not establish directions at any cost but should provide standards of precision and, along with these, levels of comparison for different conceptions and inquiries.

<h1 style="text-align:center">VI</h1>

The conceptual formulation must restrict itself with the greatest possible economy to the formal contours of certain structures. Only thus does it attain sufficient openness for intercultural and historical analysis. Above all, subjective *role-relationship,* the relationship to one's own social role and to the social role of others, must remain open.

It is precisely the subjective relationship which seems to provoke speculations which imply that certain phenomenological data are universal characteristics of the relationship of individual and role. There would be little point in discussing all the numerous proposals, which all too clearly amount to exalting highly-reflected nuances of modern subjectivity into anthropological constants. But it is instructive to follow through one particularly ingenious attempt: Georg Simmel's excursus with the strange title 'How is society possible?'.[1]

The epistemological questioning in this excursus at first links up with Kant, but then moves away from Kant until it becomes mere analogy: which processes of knowledge must — as a condition of the possibility — be postulated in order that people see, comprehend and feel themselves as belonging to a society, as a member of a social whole.[2] It can be shown that Simmel imputes certain structural characteristics of social relationships, and in particular, the inevitability of the development of role-structures. 'Society as we know it' is for him a system of roles. The question posed can accordingly be rewritten: by virtue of what processes of knowledge can we comprehend ourselves as a part, as a member of a system of differentiated roles?

Two of Simmel's arguments are of particular interest here. Both group themselves around descriptions of phenomenological data which are imputed to be universally

1 Georg Simmel, 'Wie ist Gesellschaft möglich?', *Soziologie,* 4 (1958), 21-30.
2 'See', 'understand', 'feel': therewith may be given the range within which Simmel's questioning — according to the *conditions* of these experiences — varies.

valid. 'We see the other not purely as an individual, but as a colleague or friend or party-member, in short, as a fellow inhabitant of the same special world, and this unavoidable, wholly automatically-operative, assumption is one of the means of transmitting his personality and reality in the imagination of the other into the quality and form required for his sociability.'[1] We do not see the other purely as an individual, even when we are guided by the 'thought of his real, absolutely individual distinctness' as a 'heuristic principle of knowledge'.[2] The other constantly appears to us in generalized social form, as an officer, a believer in Christianity, an official, a scholar or as a member of a family. The role-image distorts and obscures perception of individuality.

Simmel tries to give a reason for this phenomenological datum. 'Perfect knowledge of the individuality of the other' (which would also presuppose perfect identity of the deepest point of individuality) is denied to us in principle.[3] The attempt to construct an image of the other constantly leads us to distort, supplement and typify the true picture. Social generalization, in which we see the other as an officer, an official, etc., is merely the last in a series of such 're-formations'. However, in forcing us finally into this re-formation of social generalization, the impossibility of knowing a person's true individuality is also the reason for, and condition of, our specifically social perceptivity. Only by means of social generalization — the artificial limb of our defective knowledge of individuality — do the 'relationships which we know only as social ones' become possible.[4] Only this enables man to 'represent to himself' social differentiations. Only the veiling of the purely unique brings 'personality and reality in the imagination of the other up to the quality and form required by his sociability'. That which alone makes social life possible is thus, for Simmel, toned-down truth. What permits human co-existence is veiled understanding. Society only becomes possible by means of that which we do not want, i.e. by means of those qualities of our perceptive faculty which divert us from the knowledge of pure individuality; these qualities bring about what we do not wish for, in order to make possible what we must wish for: society as a relationship between socially generalized persons.

A second consideration of Simmel's in a certain way limits the first. Simmel takes a step backwards again: 'Another category in which subjects perceive themselves and each other in order that, cast in this form, they can produce empirical society, may be formulated in the apparently trivial statement: each element of a group is not only part of a society, but is something more besides.'[5]

---

1 G. Simmel, *ibid.* p. 25. 'As a fellow inhabitant of the same special world': in the quoted context Simmel has in view the case of a relationship between members of the same social circle. A corresponding, 'wholly automatically operative assumption' is obviously also valid, as it says immediately following, 'for the relationships to one another of members of different social circles'.
2 G. Simmel, *ibid.* p. 25.
3 G. Simmel, *ibid.* p. 24.
4 G. Simmel, *ibid.* p. 25.
5 G. Simmel, *ibid.* pp. 25ff.

Here too, the phenomenological datum referred to is described in concrete terms:

We know of the official that he is not only an official, of the merchant that he is not only a merchant, of the officer that he is not only an officer; and this extra-social existence, his temperament and his personal destiny, his interests and the worth of his personality, however little he may modify the central fact of his official, mercantile, and military activities, each time gives him a certain nuance for each person who comes face to face with him, and interweaves his social image with extra-social imponderables. All intercourse between people inside social categories would be different if each person confronted another only as that which he is in his category at that point in time, i.e. as the bearer of a social role devolving upon him at precisely this moment.[1]

Role-relations are therefore constantly stamped by this 'besides'. There appears in the knowledge about this 'besides' as a phenomenological datum the fact that 'the individual is, as regards certain aspects, not an element of society'. And this very fact forms the 'positive condition for the fact that he is so as regards other sides of his nature: the nature of his societated being is determined or co-determined by the nature of his non-societated being'.[2]

Now it is obvious that these arguments are determined by the tension between individual and society. The assumed concept of individuality is of a non-empirical nature. A person's 'deepest point of individuality' is not reproducible for the other. This social unreality of individuality, however, helps to make up the reality of society: 'The *a priori* truth of empirical social life is, that it is not wholly social.'[3] Both lines of thought meet in the assertions about phenomenological data in an 'on the one hand/on the other hand' situation: on the one hand, we never succeed in seeing the other person without the social generalization which corresponds to role-relation; on the other hand, the social relationship is never wholly stamped by the role-image; 'extra-social imponderables' and the knowledge of a 'besides' constantly add their resonances — and indeed in such a way that this 'besides' and this 'beyond' on the whole co-determine relations. Or in one sentence: 'All intercourse between people inside social categories would be different' if we could establish *purely* individual, or *purely* social relations.

Beyond this speculation, which formulates a certain social consciousness in a peculiarly fascinating way, there remain two statements which can count as general characterizations of subjective role-relationship. Simmel's 'social generalization' overlaps with a facet of the previously mentioned processes of social abstraction, i.e. the subsuming of individual persons under positional categories. This capacity is, as Simmel has seen, a condition for the perception of role-differentiated behaviour, a condition of social relations 'as we know them'. It must further be noted that

1   G. Simmel, *ibid.* p. 26.
2   G. Simmel, *ibid.* p. 26.
3   G. Simmel, *ibid.* p. 27. In Simmel's work the question 'How is society possible?' has the constant accompanying overtone of the secondary meaning: How is society tolerable for individuality (which sees itself as modern)?

relations between role occupants are not completely determined, or put more cautiously, must not be completely determined, by this abstraction. The omnipresence of 'imponderables' which Simmel describes, is a question of plausibility. (Moreover, he can only call them 'extra-social' because in this argument he equates 'social being' with 'role' and thus builds a bridge for himself in order to intercalate his dualism of 'societated being' and 'non-societated being' in the phenomenological datum of social relations at all.)

Whether an attempt to formulate general statements about subjective role-relationships can go beyond Simmel, we can leave undecided – in any event, the *conceptual formulation* ought to remain open to comparative analysis of the most diverse contents.

Certainly, the most diverse *classifications* of possible role-relationships may be evolved. Thus it is perhaps natural to sub-divide 'adoption' of one's *own* social role (Simmel deals only with relation to the roles of *others*) according to the traditional dialectical pattern: (1) unproblematic, spontaneous identification of the individual with his social role (implying separation of role and individual as a juxtaposition and confrontation of existence reflected in the individual and alientated – 'existing for others'); (2) the unity achieved of the two, as individualization still in accordance with role, and as the individual stamping of role.[1] Such classifications owe their attraction to historico-philosophical analogies. They are hardly a suitable starting-point for inter-cultural comparisons. Generally they only repeat the perception that there is 'something' here with which the individual can, but does not have to, identify.

Not only subjective role-relationship remains open to comparative analysis, but obviously also such variables as methods of role-allocation, the degree of role-differentiation, and the manner of role-summation. If this is overlooked then it is indeed natural to reproach role-analysis with 'a methodological blindness' in principle 'to the historical character of society'.[2] Jürgen Habermas who has raised

---

[1] Here we should, of course, think not merely of a process of adaptation of individual and role, but also of that which Simmel, in a third line of thought in his excursus, calls the 'generality-value of individuality' (pp. 28ff.). The process of allocation of positions imputes – 'not psychologically, but phenomenologically' – a fundamental 'harmony' between the supply of dissimilar individuals and the supply of dissimilar positions. 'From this standpoint the *a priori* fact now becomes visible . . . which means to the individual a basis for, and the "possibility" of, belonging to a society. That each individual, from his point of view, is assigned according to his qualities to a certain position in this social milieu; that this place which ideally belongs to him, actually exists in the social whole – this is the assumption , from which the individual lives his social life and which one can term as the generality-value of individuality.' This general thought could be translated into a problem of social psychology and social structure. It preserves us, perhaps more than other criteria, from the modern temptation to consider the fulfilment of social roles as the product of a duel between individual and role. 'That the individuality of the individual finds a place in the general structure, indeed, that this structure to a certain extent aims at this and at absorbing its particular contribution from the outset, in spite of the incalculability of individuality': this imputation, its nature and certainty, is probably more fundamental than the 'individualization with role' and 'individual stamping of role' which have been mentioned.

[2] Jürgen Habermas, *Theorie und Praxis*, p. 175.

this objection, states at once in very general terms: 'With the operational introduction of this category it (role-analysis) opens up whole spheres of social behaviour for close analysis, and must admittedly impute the "en-roled" character of society.'[1] Obviously the main point here is what one wishes to understand under the term 'en-roled character'. Unquestionably, the systematic separation of individuality and role, which has just been mentioned, is a specifically modern phenomenon. And unquestionably there have developed in industrial societies special methods of role-allocation and characteristic forms of role-differentiation and role-summation:

It is the multiplication, autonomization, and accelerated turn-over in superseded behaviour-patterns which first give 'roles' their quasi-objective existence over against the persons who 'renounce' themselves in them, and who in this self-renunciation of which they are becoming conscious, evolve the demand for inwardness — as the history of middle-class consciousness shows, especially in the 18th Century.[2]

These developments are probably a condition of modern sociological reflection about the phenomenon of role. (The questions which this raises with regard to issues in the 'sociology of knowledge' are admittedly difficult to grasp — precisely here, by way of exception, it is not sufficient to bury the explanation in the arcanum of American society.) But what does this imputed 'en-roled character of society' mean for Habermas? Unexpectedly he lets it coincide with the 'multiplication' just described and with the 'self-renunciation' of which people are becoming conscious:

Is it (role-category), however, when applied to social relationships merely generalized into a world-historical category; must role-analysis, conditioned as it is by history, altogether ignore social development as being historical, as if it were no concern of individuals whether they are subsumed like the serf of the High Middle Ages in a few natural roles, or else, perhaps, like the employee in the industrially advanced civilization, subsumed in roles which have been multiplied, which change at an accelerating rate, and which are, in a certain sense, superseded?[3]

Let us pass over the question of how natural the roles of the serf in the Middle Ages may have appeared to the serf himself. The changes which Habermas points out here, belong in any event to those problems for whose 'exact analysis' role-category must be used. It would be a thoroughly foolish undertaking indeed if 'roles as such . . . were to be immovably fixed in their constellation with role bearers?[4]

The objection can indeed, and should, always assume a new form. For it is a fact that role-analysis sees historical development as the 'modification of basic relationships which are always identical'.[5] We have attempted to formulate these basic

1   Jürgen Habermas, *ibid.* p. 173.
2   Jürgen Habermas, *ibid.* p. 174.
3   Jürgen Habermas, *ibid.* p. 174.
4   Jürgen Habermas, *ibid.* p. 174.
5   Jürgen Habermas, *ibid.* p. 174.

relationships. But, as always happens, such imputations remain questionable, and ought to be called in question.

VII

In the framework of *sociological theories* (in the narrower sense) the concept of role is no more and no less important than some other concepts. It can serve to formulate that which is to be explored (e.g. How can the change in the family role-structure be explained in the light of equality of rights?), it can fix the initial conditions, and finally it can be used in the thesis itself. The concept of role does not of itself have any explicatory value. Its function in this connection consists in detaching general comparable and precisely-defined criteria from a profusion of phenomena.

But in this sense too its usefulness is limited. The concept of role is based on a relatively far-advanced level of institutionalization. Many phenomena of societation it comprehends only peripherally. Thus, for example, it comprehends social differentiations of a non-normative type only in so far as they are connected with the framework of role-structures. In whole spheres of sociological problems its applicability remains rather limited, e.g. for analysis of class conflicts.[1]

Now the constructs which role-analysis can offer sociological theory may be subsumed under two categories: firstly, definite propositions can be based on *roles,* or rather, role-structures, and methods of role-allocation (e.g. on the relationship of social change and certain methods of role-allocation; of economic basis and family role-structures; of roles of the superior and the prospect of gaining personal authority). Further, propositions can be formulated about *behaviour* in conformity with role, or else deviating behaviour (e.g. about the relationship of position-prestige and role-conformity; of deviating behaviour and the degree of behavioural information that the norm-sender has or might have). To me it appears to be an important advantage of role-analysis that it makes possible statements about roles *and* about behaviour, be it in conformity with, or deviating from, role. This possibility can be traced back to the fact that the conceptual formulation establishes a dual classification — the extraction of certain action-sequences (of behaviour *relevant* to role) from the continuum of social behaviour, in particular also from the profusion of standardizations, and the separation of behaviour relevant to role, into conforming and deviating actions. In this way, within the same frame of reference, definitions of spheres of action which in a society stand under a

---

1 Certainly, as Dahrendorf emphasizes (p. 60), the conflict between worker and *entrepreneur* is not necessarily of personal kind, but 'given in the structure'. But this structural datum appears to me extremely imperfect, and peripherally determined by the fact that both are 'bearers of social roles', which (among other things) are defined by contradictory role-expectations. It will scarcely be possible to manage here without the (in sociology) sacred concept of interest, and it will further have to be remembered that role-norms can impose themselves which are aimed precisely at making people blind to their own interests.

particular *pressure* to conform, become possible and also differentiated statements about the *degree* of conformity. This link might be, both analytically and theoretically, especially promising. Therefore Dahrendorf's suggestion, that questions of conformity be delegated *en bloc* to psychology, to me does not appear very opportune. Of course, there would be little point in arguing about such ways of assigning spheres of competence. Dahrendorf's proposal only becomes dangerous because of the premises which underlie it: the question of behavioural conformity should be covered, in the sphere of sociology, by the equation of role and role-conforming behaviour. At the beginning of all research and theory in modern sociology would stand the statement: 'Man behaves as befits his role.' And even more clearly: 'Sociological theories rest on the assumption that social roles can be equated with human behaviour.' 'For the sociologist roles are irreducible elements of analysis.'[1] This is the genesis of Dahrendorf's 'Homo Sociologicus'. And at the same time, the genesis of a problem which derives from this equation: for the sociologist there inevitably follows what is 'almost an antithesis between his construction, which is productive for the aims of theory' – *homo sociologicus* as a man who, on principle, acts in accordance with his role – 'and his idea of human nature'.[2] One could also say: and his common sense. But why should the construction of *homo sociologicus* be productive? In my opinion it is first and foremost unnecessary. Either we formulate theoretical statements about roles and role-structures – when nothing compels us to assume simultaneously that people behave in conformity with their roles (and nothing prevents us from merely leaving this question open) – or we formulate statements about behaviour which conforms to, or deviates, from the role, and then we *put* the question of conformity. Strange to say, in the German discussion Dahrendorf's imputation has been expressly or tacitly accepted.[3] Correspondingly this conformity hypothesis was mixed up with the general discussions of possible conformity effects of sociological theory. Now, nobody really doubts that these problems exist and that, with the increasing public impact of sociology, they are being increasingly intensified. But they are on the wrong track here. *Homo sociologicus,* with all his behavioural conformity, and however frightening he may appear, is a construction which meets no sort of need even within the limits of sociology. On the contrary, it covers over again one part of the prospect which role-analysis in its initial form opens up.

One could object that statements about role-structures impute implicitly a certain frequency of appropriate behaviour. Certainly this is correct. In so far as

---

1   Jürgen Habermas, *Theorie und Praxis,* p. 77 and note to p. 45.
2   Jürgen Habermas, *ibid.* p. 87.
3   Even Tenbruck, the most method-conscious critic, seems to accept this conformity hypothesis. Possibly it has also often been overlooked that *homo sociologicus* in Dahrendorf's sense, is not man as a role-player, but man as someone who in principle acts in conformity with his role. It is only out of *this* imputation that the moral and political problems arise which Dahrendorf discusses.

such statements as we suggest, orientate themselves primarily by detectable action-sequences, they are dependent upon the detectability of certain frequencies.[1] In principle considerable possibilities still offer themselves for refining the analysis of validity-structures of norms and role-norms — possibilities of extending sociological analysis and sociological theories as well. But as long as no assertions about the validity of role-norms are made, it serves little purpose to replace the missing information by the assumption of one hundred per cent conformity.

More difficult to define is the function of the concept of role within the framework of *sociological theory in the wider sense,* i.e. of the 'Theory of Society'. S. F. Nadel has been particularly cautious in his formulation of the task facing such a theory: it is to evolve a body of propositions

which serve to map out the problem and thus prepare the ground for its empirical investigation by appropriate methods. More precisely, the propositions serve to classify phenomena, to analyse them into relevant units or indicate their interconnections, and to define 'rules of procedure' and 'schemas of interpretations'.[2]

It should immediately be clear that role-analysis is able to perform just this task. Its special advantage lies unquestionably in the fact that it aims from the start at the analysis of 'interrelationships' between 'relevant units', and therefore at the representation of structure. Nadel's list should merely be supplemented to the effect that a conceptual framework of this type attempts to produce elementary constructs, building-stones for sociological theories in the narrower sense.

These are questions of a preparatory constructive task. Now, at the end of the 'Theory of social structure' Nadel says much less cautiously, in the course of the development and application of an abstract conception of this type we arrive at a penetrating insight 'into the working of society'.[3] Insight into the functioning, mechanism, mode of work, or movement of society? The formulation is characteristic; we meet it in similar form again and again in the literature of theoretical sociology. What is actually being claimed here?

Surely, we exclude the interpretation that, simply, a claim is imputed as to the sheer reality of the conceptual framework (although in this respect Nadel, in particular, goes unusually far). Also, everything points towards the fact that this is not merely a question of a metaphorical turn of phrase which, if things 'get serious', would be retracted immediately. Paraphrasing this, one might well say that in such formulations there comes to light the tendency not just to understand a general sociological theory as a preliminary to more specifically theoretical statements, but also to make it fast by the other end — as a continuation and part of social anthropology.

But this tendency mostly receives only cautious formulation; it is more hinted at than expressed. Thus in the conception of fundamental sociological concepts its

[1] See above, section V.
[2] S. F. Nadel, *The Theory of Social Structure,* p. 1.
[3] S. F. Nadel, *ibid.* p. 154.

effect is rather confusing, and creates the ambivalence and uncertainty already mentioned at the beginning.

Let us therefore ask more straightforwardly, what is actually imputed when insights 'into the working of society' are spoken of? The imputation is, that people who form themselves into a society impose rules upon themselves, and create sets of order. The imputation is further that they do this in an extremely artificial way, as artificially as making fire, inventing tools, using language. Finally it is imputed that the *artificium* of society can be in form infinitely variable as regards content, but not as regards construction. Lasting societation requires, for example, the setting-up of regularities in social behaviour on the basis of agreements about abstractions, the drawing-up of sanctionable norms, the relation of normative sub-systems to one another, and social generalization of individuals into role-bearers.

Now, these are of course strongly abstractive statements which split up connections and isolate analytically useful characteristics. It would not take us one step further if we were to maintain that with these statements — and only these — we had set down on paper '*the* working of society'. Yet we can formulate the claim that these statements do say something about how people form themselves into societies, and how society as we know it is constructed. Behind this there may be the more far-reaching thought that it is a question here of conditions of possibility of societation. In the light of formal logic this thought might be given concrete form in a model of premisses and deductions. Methodologically, however, it takes us further if we can show that with the help of basic sociological concepts statements may be formulated about social structures which can lay claim to *universal validity*. These statements relate themselves therefore to 'society' in the sense of '*all* societies' which we know. At the same time it is possible to introduce qualifications such as the limitation to complete societies or to the processes of societation which have reached a certain level of permanence and stability. Obviously these statements would be empty if they were not refutable. The question therefore is constantly whether the case where refutation does occur can be fixed sufficiently unequivocally. As far as the concept of role is concerned — in the form developed here — we can give an affirmative answer to this question.

The claim to universality would — according to our deduction — be refuted if a complete society could be found in which no behavioural regularities were identifiable which, in the event of deviating behaviour, would be reinforced by means of sanctioning reactions; a complete society in which behavioural regularities of this kind were not tied — with different contents respectively — to different classes of individuals; a complete society in which for some of these classes of individuals lasting (i.e. capable of being passed on) positional valencies in society were not foreseen, and for the filling of which no provision was made. (Probably one could take a further risk here and add that constantly some of these positional valencies are also expressly *named* in the language.)

Thus, to me it appears justified when in the discussion about the concept of role, the claim crops up again and again that with this basic concept something fundamental to society is touched upon. It is only necessary to free this claim from the vague to-ing and fro-ing of cautious and risky turns of phrase, and to formulate it in a form accessible to criticism. This is done by means of the formulation of the universality thesis. If a theory of society is built up as a series of such universality theses, then it does not only prepare the way for special sociological theories, but it also gives a general and verifiable insight into the social conditions of men.

The universality thesis does not, however, only define a claim to generality which is usually put vaguely. It also gives conceptual considerations a clear frame of reference. These considerations must aim at comparability. (Thus in our case, for example, the comparability of statements about different systems of role-allocation, role-accumulation, and role-structure.) This, however, should provoke the question as to how far the bow of comparability is to be bent at any one time. If it is possible to form concepts with which verifiable statements about universal phenomena of human societation and their modifications may be formulated, then the frame of reference of comparability is in no way less exactly, but more exactly, denoted than usual. This claim, however, reacts upon the process of conceptual abstraction: it is given a clear aim, and it is subjected to a definable load-test. This is the explanation why the concept of role, which here is orientated, *expressis verbis,* by a 'broadly' conceived task, is unusually narrowly defined.

3

THE MAN AND THE MASK:
A DISCUSSION OF ROLE-THEORY[1]

MALCOLM BRADBURY, BRYAN HEADING and
MARTIN HOLLIS

1. INTRODUCTION

Hollis: I have heard it said that a man is the sum of the roles which he plays.
Could you please explain this implausible doctrine to us?

Heading: Certainly, but I must start by telling you what I understand by 'role',
since sociologists use the term in different ways. First, I distinguish social positions
from the individuals who occupy them. You, for instance, are local secretary of
your branch of the Logicians' Union. Next year someone else may be. The
occupant will have changed and the position remained the same. In general a
social position (or 'status') is a location in a social structure, usually recognized in
the language of the members of the society. Husband, father, Catholic, dustman
and chess player are examples. An individual's 'position set' (or 'status set')
is the sum of his social positions.

Secondly, behaviour in each position is neither completely idiosyncratic nor
random. Let us *start* by calling the active dimension of a social position a 'role'.
In your role of branch secretary, for example, you collect subscriptions, organize
hair-splitting contests and notify members of them. 'Role' thus draws our attention
to any behaviour regularly emitted by the occupant of a position, behaviour that
is therefore predictable to role-partners and informed observers. It is such behaviour
that interests the role analyst and that he seeks to explain.

Hollis: You seem to imply that there is a role wherever there is predictable
behaviour. My neighbour regularly passes my door at noon each day. Yet surely it
does not follow from this alone that there is a role of neighbour. You may retort
that he does not do it *because* he is my neighbour. True enough. But he walks

[1] This article is an edited version of a discussion held between Bryan Heading (sociology),
Martin Hollis (philosophy) and Malcolm Bradbury (literary criticism) at the University of
East Anglia, Norwich, England. It benefits from discussion before an interdisciplinary faculty
group in the university; in addition, Bryan Heading would like to acknowledge his debt to
former teachers and colleagues at Columbia University, and especially Robert K. Merton and
William J. Goode. Martin Hollis's final suggestion about the place of theory in social science
is a joint one which he and Edward J. Nell of the New School, New York are currently
working out in a book on philosophy and economic theory.

predictably slowly, because he has a weak heart. Yet surely there is not therefore a role of 'man with a weak heart'?

Heading: When I have completed my discussion of the role concept I think that you will see why I do not discern a role of 'man with a weak heart', but you have raised a real problem here: precisely what are the boundaries of the subject-matter of the role analyst? When do human activities become sufficiently distinctive and structured to warrant description in terms of social positions and roles? No role analyst has yet developed definitive criteria of what represents a social position and while this is regrettable, and perhaps particularly disturbing for the philosopher, it does not in my opinion completely undermine the role orientation.

Hollis: Another snag of assigning all predictable behaviour to a role is that the notion of 'role' becomes otiose. There surely has to be a revealing difference between 'It is in the role of neighbour to be kind to the children next door' and 'All (or most) neighbours are kind to children next door'. Otherwise you may as well drop talk of roles; science is not made by jargon alone.

Heading: I agree; and the role analyst is interested in a special brand of predictable behaviour. This brings me on to the third element in my definition: 'role' describes the rights and obligations which are inherent in the occupancy of a social position, the norms or moral rules which define the behaviour that you are entitled to receive from your role-partners and that you should engage in with them. To the extent that there is agreement about the content of the norms and that people live up to them, legitimate expectations about the behaviour of role-partners will be upheld. But it is possible, of course, that there may not be complete agreement, either amongst the incumbents of a position or amongst their role-partners, on the normative content, and it is equally possible that, even with normative consensus, some people will fail to live up to expectations.

Hollis: The key word here is 'entitled' – a moral word. Role behaviour not so much 'is' as 'morally ought to be' predictable, in the sense that failure to conform is rightly open to criticism. Have I understood you?

Heading: Absolutely. It is clear that, if we define role in terms of normative expectations (my preferred definition), not all expected behaviour need contain an element of moral requirement, hence the 'role' is a subset of all expected behaviour. Moreover, as you rightly observe, actual behaviour ('role behaviour') may not fall into line with normative expectations and such 'deviation', whether expected or not, is open to criticism or worse. But we must remember that my notion of 'moral' is social and not absolute. To discover what a role-player ought to do we consult not God but social custom.

May I make a final definitional point here? Some role analysts, following Robert Merton, use the term 'role' to refer to the normative expectations governing the relationship between a position-incumbent and role-partners occupying a *particular* position, e.g. role of teacher in relationship with students. Then each social position has an array of such roles associated with it, the 'role set'. Thus the teacher has roles governing his relationships with administrators, parents, fellow teachers as well as students. I accept the usefulness of this perspective, with its implied suggestion that different role-partners may have different and conflicting expectations of the position-incumbent, but I do not think it essential to hold to it rigorously in the discussion that follows.

Hollis: So much for definitions. A man's behaviour, then, is to be explained at least partly in terms of normative expectations belonging to his social positions. But what about the *playing* of roles?

2. THE THEATRICAL ANALOGY

Heading: I hope that I have made it clear that 'role' is a core concept for the sociologist, one used explicitly or implicitly by those studying small groups or large organizations, and by those focusing on social conflict as well as by those who stress social consensus. It represents a link between individual personality and social structure, since the individual actor as role-player performs on the stage of the broader society. It is because the individual plays roles that there is a discipline of sociology at all; roles are an 'emergent' property not understandable in terms of the qualities of individuals alone but developing out of the interaction of individuals in particular environmental settings and which then influence the behaviour of these individuals and possible future generations who are socialized or constrained to employ them. It is because individuals are role-players that their behaviour is neither idiosyncratic nor random.

You will have noticed that I described the relationship between individual and social structure by analogy with the theatre, an analogy which has inspired the development of role analysis. The social actor, then, resembles the stage actor, The latter is, so to speak, programmed. He operates with a script written for him which he has learnt at some point in the past, emitting cues which elicit responses from other actors, many of which he has already anticipated; indeed his earlier cues were designed to elicit those responses. He is motivated to follow the script, to comply with the rules of the game. Such motivation to conform with the norms results from having already internalized a moral commitment to comply (the Freudian super-ego equivalent) or from a desire for reward from the rest of the cast, director, audience and critics that is dependent on conformity (Freud's ego-operation) or from both these processes. When he fails through being badly cast, forgetful or whatever, he must accept guilt-feelings and/or negative sanctions from his role-partners unless he can persuade them to modify their expectations.

Bradbury: I wonder how far we can press the dramaturgical analogy? If it is to be truly illuminating, we should be able to elaborate and examine the metaphor. I had better say that the role-theorist who has most interested me is Erving Goffman, since he seems to me to be concerned with the dramatic nature of our social and cultural transactions and is capable of seeing them, as literature does, both from an individual and a social point of view. Now Goffman exploits the metaphor in a very distinctive way, I suppose a very literary way. He thinks, as I see it, of society as a stage on which we enter to play our parts; life, social life, is 'the games people play' and they know they are playing them — they come on for a span and then withdraw. They are actors in the sense of being *personae*; they assume masks, albeit obviously powerful ones; they enact some salient action or movement or, better, transaction in the society; and then they are permitted to retire into some more real self — like waiters who lose part of their role as waiters when they pass through the swing-doors into the kitchen. Now already this seems to diverge from your account of role, which is a good deal less personalized, and I take it you are exploiting this crucial analogy somewhat differently. For instance, you are putting less weight on the transaction, the social dialogue, and more on society as a total theatre.

Heading: Yes, I take a more cautious view of the analogy than Goffman. He presents man in a fairly introspective, self-aware manner. The merit of such an approach is that it recognizes that man is not simply a passive reflection of 'society' but an individual capable of exercising some freedom in the choice of ends and means of action. But it also tends to suggest that each of us can don and doff his roles like hats and has great autonomy within each role. The more orthodox, and plausible, view is that although different roles are articulated in different situations — for example the waiter behaves differently in the kitchen because he is interacting with different role-partners who have dissimilar relations with and expectations of him — at the same time complete compartmentalization of roles is rare. Have you never come across a waiter who is surly and touchy because things are going wrong in the kitchen? And isn't it likely that many chefs do the cooking at home where it has traditionally been the woman's role? Roles often spill over into situations other than those where they are directly applicable. A role, therefore, is more than something public to be laid down at clocking-off time.

Bradbury: So the parallel with the actor breaks down at once?

Heading: On the contrary, I suggest that the actor cannot simply don and doff roles either. He brings something of himself, and probably of his director, to his parts and, to the extent that he becomes immersed in his parts, he takes something of them into himself.

Bradbury: There are two different accounts of acting. One takes the actor to personify Lear; the other takes him to impersonate, to become for a time, Lear. These are two opposite implications of the metaphor that all the world's a stage. Impersonation, becoming Lear, has long been regarded with a kind of terror; it's been thought dangerous to the actor because it involves a sacrifice of his essential self. Well, I don't want to insist on the concept of the essential self too much, since I grant that we are all social creatures. But all the same something of this kind of terror carries over into my response to role-theory. Hence the question I want to raise is how far, in your role as role-theorist, you hold society to be *in* man and how, if at all, the social self is distinct from the private self. In other words, I am asking about the psychology of role-playing. To illustrate my point: a good deal of literature, especially fiction and drama, concerns itself with the intercourse between man and society. Yet it very typically approaches society from the standpoint of the individual experiencing it, and shows him in the position of a sceptic, exploring the world of position-sets, rewards and expectations you have been talking about, yet only accepting those that acquire a pragmatic or moral validity. Man is both a sceptic and an innovator; he can make social experience anew within obvious limits. What I'm talking about is very recognizable in the novel generally; it's usually recognized that a recurrent feature of the form is that it contains this empirical scepticism — which is one reason why sociologically-orientated critics talk about it as a bourgeois form. But for that matter you can find the same sort of emphasis in most drama, which tends to enquire into the relationship between roles and realities. And I suspect that what literature has to say on the matter of role — admittedly it may be defining the word differently, but I'm not sure about that — is in the direction of an humanistic individualism. Now in my own role, as writer and as critic, I share that bias. What I want to know is whether you are discounting it.

Heading: Your values are clear and you practise them professionally. The sociologist may also be personally inspired by humanistic individualism but, in his professional role, he tries to describe and explain regularities in human behaviour. Like astronomy, physics, economics, psychology or any other science, sociology is a generalizing subject. The sociologist has concluded that human regularities largely result from what you call 'impersonation', that is the taking into one's self of values, attitudes, expected patterns of behaviour originating outside one's self. You appear to work with some notion of 'natural man', born with a personality suitable for parading on the world-stage, and with happiness or 'self-realization' following from a minimum of social intervention. Although many young radicals, including some sociologists, appear to share this notion, most sociologists regard it as a myth and a dangerous one. Our view of man suggests a minimal instinctual apparatus and a state of social and personal 'nothingness' at birth, less 'original sin' than 'original anomie'! And although you might suggest that you are aiming only at the exercise of individualism by already socialized men, the sociologist asks how individualism stops short of anarchy and, if you are supportive of an anarchic situation, what institutional safeguards are required to stop anarchy becoming a man-made Hobbesian world?

Bradbury: Well, let me clarify my point a bit there, since I'm not really arguing that way at all. My point is that, where the sociologist tends to emphasize the concept of normative behaviour, literature, which is a characteristically empirical species of curiosity, tends to stress the elements of scepticism and self-assessment that go into the assumption of roles. Tom Jones may take up the role of squire at the end of Fielding's novel, but he doesn't take it up in the way that Squire

Allworthy does: he has been through a kind of empirical moral examination of the dangers and risks of the role. Now you say that the value of the concept of role is that it represents the link between the individual personality and the social structure; its danger, it seems to me, is that it is a way of projecting society into the individual without being a way of projecting the individual into society. Hence my unease about the way the analogy with the theatre is being employed.

Hollis: If I might come in – no wonder, Bryan, you think a man the sum of his roles! 'Natural man', you imply, is a nugget of anti-social instinct, who gains his later identity from social institutions. *Homo sociologicus,* as you seem to see him, is the destructive offspring of Hobbes' *Leviathan,* stewed in the syrup of the Enlightenment. Where Helvetius says, 'It does not matter whether men are good or bad – law is everything', you add only that without law they are bad. I protest. I accept neither Hobbes' notion nor Helvetius' and, in any case, I doubt whether they can be combined. While wholly agreeing that some theory about 'human nature' will be integral to sociology, I must ask if you mean to insist on that one.

Heading: Not so fast! I was only trying to contrast the literary orientation with the sociological. But having introduced an important digression, I should comment briefly on the idea of 'a man-made Hobbesian world'. If individuals have been socialized to have great and expanding wants and if they are now encouraged to view critically existing restraints upon the means used to satisfy these wants and to 'do their own thing', then we may well create through social action relationships of the type that Hobbes, mistakenly, thought were a consequence of man's nature.

However, I am not meaning to deny the existence of a private self which may, should and does influence an individual's role-playing. I shall examine the place of the individual in role-analysis later. But I am suggesting that, in social life, 'impersonation' is always important by choice of the individual actor or as a necessary means to rewards from role-partners. However, the extent to which intrusion of self in role-playing is encouraged clearly varies: many roles like those of nurse or dentist, have rigid norms designed to exclude the rest of the self and, as you know, the norms of actors vary from the traditionalism of the Kabuki theatre, to the stylized individualism of 'Hair', to almost completely unstructured group happenings; the reception accorded these different styles of acting largely depends upon the expectations of audience and critics.

Bradbury: Let us press a bit further with the theatrical analogy, since I begin to suspect the way you are using it. At first it seemed that you were applying it mainly to suggest that man is an *actor,* who comes forward to play certain parts on the stage of society. But that notion tends to involve a notion of human independence; he can act or not. And so you have moved in the direction of suggesting that man is, rather, a *character* – someone irretrievably within the play. Now an actor and a character exist in worlds that we presume to be totally differently ordered. The actor leaves the stage; the character really may not do so. The actor belongs to the same world as the author, and participates in the making of a fiction; the character is in a closed world. Lear has never heard of Shakespeare; he has never taken part in rehearsals; he does not know what Goneril is about to do. But the author and actor do know all these things. The events of the play are programmed, but the assumption of the characters is that they are happening here for the first and only time. All this is in the nature of the predicate of the play. But I would be uneasy about saying that this is what social life is like.

Heading: Perhaps we are stretching the analogy too far, though I agree that, if it is going to be used as a basic metaphor in sociology, it should merit elaboration. Your point is, of course, correct — the characters in social role-theory must be seen as engaging in relationships without any idea that the next scene has been predetermined. Yet in all their interaction the sociologist thinks he can detect the social play being enacted. Important aspects of their friendships and conflict are patterned. Direct or indirect reference is usually made to the rights and obligations governing such relationships as father and daughter, king and courtier, whether in plays or real life.

Bradbury: Well, on this I agree with you, though I think you are picking out particular aspects of the idea of a play. In all literature we can recognize that people do play roles; and Aristotle, for instance, suggests the main action of a play is social — you can have, he says, a play without individual characters, characters with distinct personal motives, or significant course of action. But in fact this tends towards the literary stereotype, the routine and under-created figure that we recognize normally as a signal of bad and easy writing. And a good deal of literature is organized according to the very different principle of presenting the fictional action through the characters, which are given in depth and are prior. 'Society' thus becomes a dramatization of the needs of self when it seeks interaction with others. Now my point isn't just that you need to have a sense of the individual as a power in order to write good plays or novels. It is that drama and literature have quite elaborate notions of role as an aspect of fictional creation. But normally these involve an understanding of the complexity of the relationship between patterned expectations, social constraints, and the psychological needs and creative powers of individuals. To take a specific example for a minute — and to take it from the novel, since it does get us out of the confusion induced by the fact that in plays there are two kinds of actors, the performers playing parts and the characters whose parts they play. In, for instance, Jane Austen's *Emma* it is quite clear that an elaborate social fabric is constructed in the novel, involving a world limited by social constraints and particular areas of option. All these are part of the normal fictional world of the book, part of the novelist's general description; these are the novel's 'society'. But within that, role is then interpreted as a specific framework which defines the creative options of the characters. What I'm saying is that there seems to me a marked difference between the idea of social constraint, which is one definition of role, and the human performance as a possibility, a possibility enabled by the larger expectations for himself he can explore within accepted limitations.

I'm arguing, if you like, for the notion of role as a body of social constraints and institutionalized relationships in terms of which each individual acts creatively. But you are seeing man as the roles that he plays. I would say, therefore, that you are misusing the analogy with the theatre and literature, and misusing the metaphor. Where a role is a mask, you are making it a face as well. The paradoxes within the metaphor enable you to do this, precisely because of the curious ambiguity of theatre. But it can become the instrument for a slightly disturbing imperialism whereby the actor is explained only in terms of the play he is in.

Heading: As you recognize, a play *can* be viewed from many perspectives. A sociologist could indeed examine it in terms of role-relationships and role-conflict of the characters. He could, and perhaps should, also examine it from the perspective of the author. Since the Renaissance, most playwrights have insisted on the individual's freedom to control events; indeed I do not think I am being too outrageous in suggesting that modern dramatists see this as part of their role, along with directors and actors. Role-theorists hold a more mediaeval dramatical view and although I regard the modern playwright's perspective, which you appear to share, as an overstatement of real-life situations, it is a timely reminder to many sociologists, who tend to think of men as much more programmed and passive than do playwrights, to examine systematically the impact of individual personality upon role-playing, especially in situations and general cultures which encourage individuality. Incidentally, an interesting synthesis of the perspectives of the dramatist and the role-analyst is produced by the writer of 'soap operas' and 'kitchen sink' plays, who portrays his characters responding to their situations in both stereotyped and 'individualistic' ways.

3. THE INDIVIDUAL IN ROLE-ANALYSIS

Hollis: In upshot, then, it is no use appealing to the metaphor of the theatre to explain in what sense a man is the sum of the roles which he plays. For the metaphor simply raises the questions, or, at best, gives them conflicting answers. Is *all* the world a stage? When the actor removes his last mask, is there a face beneath? There are several possible and conflicting accounts of the nature of drama and you are not entitled to assume one of them just because it supports your view of man. Your general thesis, I suppose, is that the individual stands to the actor as the actor stands to the character in the play. But, for all your earlier talk of a 'private self', does role-theory have any possible place for the individual?

Heading: Certainly role-theory has a place for the individual personality. Both Georg Simmel and G. H. Mead recognized that modern man can be examined in terms of all the roles associated with social positions presently occupied, along with some precipitates of positions occupied in the past and, possibly, some aspects of positions with which the individual identifies without actually occupying them, the last being non-membership reference-models. The diversity of these roles for different individuals is surely a major source of individuality.

Bradbury: Suggesting that the man *is* the mask?

Heading: Within the limits of orthodox role analysis yes, although I prefer not to use your language since the 'mask' is part of the individual's real experience. But we must not be naive. There are at least four other factors that I would want to consider, though perhaps these should be seen as the province of the biologist, psychologist and social psychologist.

First, a man has a 'genotype' and a developed body which presumably influence all of his behaviour. The exact importance of genetical factors is, of course, disputed — how much 'nature' is there in the nature—nurture dichotomy? Those with forty-seven chromosomes, for instance, appear to be more aggressive than others by nature but social factors determine the particular form the aggression takes and, possibly, whether it is turned inward or outward. When Dennis Wrong says 'In the beginning is the body' and describes man as 'socialized but only partly so' he implies that there are forces in man unamenable to socialization without adequately suggesting what they are or how important they may be in total behaviour.

Secondly, a man comes to play his roles in a peculiar way because of the *particular* role-partners he has been socialized by and interacts with. Mead, in my opinion, does not adequately tackle the problem of how individuals move from the 'particular other' to a shared conception of the 'generalized other'. Individuals probably have different conceptions of the content of a role because they have been influenced by different role-partners, and the role analyst, in concentrating on the 'generalized other', neglects individual variations on the theme.

Thirdly, a man probably tries to develop a coherent sense of self. Admittedly we are not all equally introspective and do not all feel an equal need for an internally consistent personality. Some of us 'compartmentalize' contradictory roles either within a single social position (e.g. the university lecturer, whose colleagues expect devotion to research and whose students expect devotion to teaching) or between social positions (e.g. the homosexual who, after a night on the town with 'the boys', returns home to wife and children). Although most social psychologists detect a 'a strain towards consistency', many individuals do not succeed in being consistent and may compartmentalize effectively if the conflicting situations can be kept separate in time, place and role-partners, and if awareness of the contradictions does not produce schizophrenia. But the individual can be expected to minimize status conflict to the extent that he can exercise 'self-selection' over positions occupied — presumably the convinced Christian Scientist would not choose to become a doctor! Now to the extent that the individual does develop a coherent personality he will carry it into all his role-acting situations and there is likely to be 'spill-over' of elements of personality developed in other social contexts into the role being articulated now (e.g. the businessman who treats friends in cost-accounting terms).

Fourthly, as I mentioned earlier, an important part of personality consists of values, attitudes and patterns of behaviour learnt in the past, retained, and affecting present and future action. The psychologist, whether Freudian or Skinnerian, is particularly interested in explaining which of all past behaviour patterns are retained. The sociologist is interested insofar as they are the outcome of past role-relationships (e.g. Freud's analysis of the Oedipus complex might be reinterpreted as the effect of raising a young boy in a patriarchal nuclear family with a taboo on mother—son sex relations).

So I admit the complexities of the individual personality. Not only does it have a 'nature' dimension, but its 'nurture' dimension contains elements usually examined by psychologists and social psychologists, as well as the role aspect which is the particular province of the sociologist.

Hollis: But does that answer the question? I asked, 'Does role-theory have any possible place for the individual?' and your reply began, 'Certainly role-theory has a place for the individual personality'. But are you entitled to equate individuals with individual personalities? You are presumably suggesting that what makes an individual unique is that he is the only person who combines his set of roles with his genotype, phenotype, and previous role-partners and experiences. You must take this line, I think, because, as you put it, 'Sociology is a generalizing subject'. In other words, you must be able to formulate all your conclusions as scientific laws in universal statements. So you must be able to generalize about individuals, by saying (however specious it sounds) that *all* individuals with just that role-set, nature and nurture will behave in such and such a way in such and such conditions. The individual personality is the only instance of a law about the intersection of a complex of laws.

Now that account, whether or not it is the truth, is not how most men think of themselves. They like to fancy that they are men of decision, owners of experience and captains of their souls. In this sense the individual is whatever has the personality, wears the mask and plays the roles. The individual is active; the individual personality is passive. The former innovates; the latter has innovations thrust upon it. I suppose you regard this notion of self as mistaken. But, in that case, what is your sociological account of the innovating individual?

4. INNOVATION AND ROLE-ANALYSIS

Heading: I agree that sociologists often treat the actor as if he was passive. They see him strictly as *homo sociologicus,* playing out roles learnt in the past, moulded by society. This picture of man cannot explain social change as the result of human initiative. But a minority of role-analysts do see man as an active agent. G. H. Mead, for example, recognized that man's personality involves an innovating agent, the 'I', as well as the 'me', the outcome of role-relationships, and that the 'I' does not always do what the 'me' suggests. But, in my opinion, he failed to explain adequately the discrepancy between 'I' and 'me'; so let me try to improve upon his account.

First, as I have shown above, a sophisticated role-analysis allied with psychology and biology does have a place for the individual personality which influences all role-playing. From the point of view of a particular individual, his action may not be innovative but a part of his basic personality, but in interaction with others he may have innovative *social* consequences, especially if he occupies a position of power or authority. Thus a 'strong' Prime Minister chooses colleagues as Cabinet Ministers who he expects to support him and 'persuades' them to propose new legislation on labour relations which is accepted by the House of Commons, although conceivably a majority of members privately disagree with it; such legislation may occasionally be the result of the actions and beliefs of a tiny number of men, even a single one, in strategic places.

Secondly, within role-analysis itself there are some clues to the reasons for innovative behaviour. An individual may have been inadequately socialized and therefore not know what he is meant to do in a given situation. If adequately socialized, while some norms absolutely prescribe or proscribe certain types of behaviour, other norms are not as strongly worded nor do they involve such strong sanctions − presumably in this case the individual is not under the same pressure to conform and may engage in 'deviant' behaviour, perhaps innovative from the perspective of group members. In addition, some norms only require behaviour within certain parameters without specifying precisely what the expected behaviour is, thereby allowing plenty of leeway to the individual. Furthermore in some situations in which the individual finds himself, he receives little, if any, normative guidance (e.g. the status of divorcee) and therefore he is forced to make his own decisions; an important problem for the sociologist is why some social positions should be characterized by incomplete guide-lines, why they should involve 'anomic' states for the actor. A special case of a situation where the individual receives incomplete guidance for his actions is one in which his values are open-ended; as Veblen pointed out, 'status-striving' knows no limit. Under these conditions, which I describe as 'institutionalized anomie', the individual cannot attain a final goal because there is none and, therefore, he will be always searching for new ones. Another crucial point, too often neglected by many sociologists, is that the norms *may* require an individual to innovate. For example the entrepreneur portrayed by Joseph Schumpeter is enjoined by his own values to engage in new business ventures and Max Weber's Protestant believer was required to live rationally and ascetically, with the result that, if engaged in business activities, he was under constant pressure to improve his productive techniques and if, as was likely, he made profits, being unable to consume them he ploughed them back into new profitable ventures. It should not surprise us that radical critiques of society, by faculty and students, occur most often in liberal universities and in the humanities and social sciences − in such situations, people have been encouraged to engage in critical thought about the fate of man in society and have been taught to expect praise for such thought. (It is much more uncertain that they will actually receive such praise, because it will depend upon people's estimation of the 'quality' of the thought and many of their hearers, while accepting the value of critical thought in principle, may reject the results of it in practice!) I should also mention that individuals faced with role or status-conflict may engage in novel behaviour if they attempt to overcome the conflict and no generally accepted means of overcoming it exist.

Finally, the individual may innovate because he faces external situations for which he has not been 'programmed'. Such situations might involve changes in the physical environment, for example Irishmen reacting to the potato famine of the 1840s, or the stockbroker deciding to forego his umbrella during a heatwave: yet some brokers are so well 'programmed' that they continue to take their umbrellas and winter suits into the tropical sun! The situation might alternatively involve particular role-partners who behave unexpectedly for reasons mentioned above and who thereby affect our actor's behaviour. Or the individual might live in a social system in which he discovers that he cannot reach his socially legitimate goals by the 'right' means (e.g. Robert Merton's working class individual, in the article 'Social Structure and Anomie', who has been socialized to achieve an American level of success but has no real opportunity to do so and, therefore, is under pressure to use new and 'deviant' means to attain his goals).

Hollis: An impressive array of analytical tools! But they do not rob the other view of its point. Innovating is not merely doing something for the first time. For instance, Agamemnon was the first man to sacrifice his daughter to persuade the gods to send a fair wind. But that was not an innovation, since (if we take the myth at face value) his roles of king and priest required it. In other words, if we assume his action explicable by role-analysis, we must believe that his action was always implicit in his role-set, needing only an occasion to become explicit. Otherwise role-theory cannot explain why he acted as he did. But the man who does what it is in his roles to do is not innovating. On the other side of the coin, role-theory can explain why what is forbidden by the role-set is not done. Why did Oedipus not flee from Thebes, when his unwitting crime came to light? Because, in his role as king, he had to keep his public vow. Role-theory must be an explanation of why what is required is done and what is forbidden is not done. This is its scope − but only if it is also its limits.

Innovation occurs either when conflicting roles are so finely balanced that no particular action is favoured or when there is more than one action neither required nor forbidden. *Ex hypothesi* role-theory cannot explain here why what was done and neither therefore can it predict what a man so placed will do. Yet these are typical examples for innovation in its 'unscientific' sense. Your own account of the factors giving rise to innovation does not create a place for innovation within role-theory but, rather, states the limits which role-theory must accept. For it shows how the theory can explain why *an* innovation occurred, while implicitly admitting that it cannot explain why the innovation took the particular form it did. I repeat that if the latter were explicable by role-theory, no innovation would be involved.

If you agree, we must look elsewhere to explain innovation. In keeping with your earlier view of man, you look next, I think, to biology, psychology or social psychology. I shall argue for another strategy later. But first can we be clear whether you think of this as an extension of sociology or as a gesture of solidarity to fellow-scientists? How ambitious are your claims for role-theory and sociology? You no doubt intend to dispute what I have just said. In principle, you might claim that role-theory explains all human behaviour or all social behaviour or only some social behaviour. Which?

5. THE SCOPE AND SCIENTIFIC NATURE OF ROLE-ANALYSIS

Heading: As I have said already, role-analysis cannot explain 'all human behaviour', because of the relevance of biology and psychology.

Hollis: Perhaps I should have said 'action' rather than behaviour. After all, it would be odd to expect sociology to explain the workings of a man's digestive system.

Heading: Besides, in the tradition of Weber and Mead, I am interested mainly in actions symbolically significant to the agent, whose explanation depends upon the agent's inner understanding of and reaction to the situation. But in no sense do I deny the importance of biological factors. Moreover I accept the insights of behavioural psychology as valid, even if it tells us too little about the content of responses and the nature of reinforcers and makes the response, in my view, seem too automatic. However, I would prefer to avoid deciding the scope of behaviourism just now! So let us agree that we are discussing significant action as opposed to physical behaviour. Role-analysis cannot, and does not claim to, explain all significant action.

Hollis: What about 'all social action'? Or, if you are equating 'social' with 'significant', which social actions does role-theory explain?

Heading: If 'social action' is defined as 'action explicable by role-analysis', the question is easily answered! But that sweeps our problem under the rug. If we agree that sociology is the study of man as a social, essentially non-instinctual, animal, the problem becomes a twofold one: what are the boundaries separating sociology from the other human sciences and what is the place of role-analysis in sociology? I cannot tackle the scope of sociology at any great length here. It has always involved a reaction against essentially individualistic notions of man, whether psychological, economic or philosophical, whether the creation of Philosophes or of Utilitarians. Sociologists have posited and demonstrated empirically to their satisfaction (the unconvinced should read or re-read Durkheim's *Suicide*) that an important component of the behaviour of individuals is the social context within which people have previously developed values, cathexes, expectations and patterns of behaviour and within which they are now being further socialized and acting to achieve their goals, a social context that offers them rewards and punishments. All contemporary sociologists share this perspective though most are careful, as I trust I have been during our discussion, not to reify the central concepts of 'group', 'society', 'norm' and 'value'.

In clarifying the relationship between sociology and psychology let me make use of a distinction developed by Max Weber when discussing the relationship between sociology and economics. He separated 'basically economic' action from 'economically relevant' and 'economically conditioned' action. Let us start by describing basically sociological action as role-playing, though since this is the rub of our second problem I shall have to re-examine it in a moment. Basically psychological action is that deriving from the personality of an individual, not systematically viewed as a result of specified social-contextual experiences. Now, as I showed in my discussion of the individual and role-analysis, psychological factors are sociologically relevant since they fundamentally influence an individual's role-playing. Even if many such factors are usually introduced by sociologists only to explain 'deviant' cases, we must remember that the explanation of 'deviant' cases is relevant to the explanation of 'normal' ones. At the same time, psychological factors are sociologically conditioned, since the individual personality is crucially influenced by past, present and anticipated future role-relationships.

Bradbury: I wonder if I could pick up a phrase you used there: 'Psychological factors are socially relevant since they fundamentally influence an individual's role-playing.' I have been silent, but worried; and what worries me is the belief I detect in what you are saying that an account of role-playing, if sufficiently full, will be a total account of man. You can subsume into it all other species of human science. Martin has been pushing you hard on this, but I think a small push should come from another direction. I said earlier that I thought that the theatrical metaphor could be used deviously, and I think the evidence grows clearer. It becomes a way of saying that all we do, we do as social actors; and you will recall that I doubted that as anything other than a convenient fiction. It is a fiction that enables sociology to claim that it is not simply studying one aspect of behaviour, but all behaviour. Society, via role, is always in man; and society, because what you are doing is sociology, is naturally prior. The idea of role thus becomes a means of sociological imperialism. Now, like Martin, I think it should be used to define the fact that sociology does have boundaries; its species of explanation reaches its limits here in a paradox, about the fact that all experience is simultaneously social and personal, and it's around here that sociology should recognize its limitations as well as its undoubted resources to offer a profound but *partial* interpretation of man.

Heading: If I go on, you will see that I don't entirely dissent from that. To add one more view of the distinctive sociological perspective, the sociologist is particularly interested in why the *rates* of suicide or innovation vary in different societies and amongst different social groups and categories at different times. We do not presume to explain every particular suicide or innovation, but believe that variable rates of behaviour are the result of variable 'group' attributes. Some of us admit that analysts who start by focusing upon particular cases may provide insights into different rates of the phenomenon and we certainly believe that our perspective gives some insight into the many factors responsible for any particular case. Thus Durkheim's sociological analysis may suggest reasons why Doris Bloggs committed suicide a month after she had won the pools, but no sociologist would expect it to provide an 'adequate' explanation.

So, even if sociology is taken as attempting to explain 'all *social* action', by definition, non-sociological factors are 'sociologically relevant', And when we come to allocating *human* action between psychology, sociology and social psychology (an uncertain hybrid, usually examining the influence of small groups or small aggregates upon the individual or vice-versa), we must recognize that although they have focused for historical reasons upon different aspects of human action, the boundaries between them are artificial and increasingly seen as such. Hence, sociology offers a *partial* explanation of human action. The philosopher would, of course, like to know *how* partial this explanation is. So would the sociologist, but just as we have shelved the question of exactly how important 'nature' and 'nurture' are, so we must recognize that dividing 'nurture' between the various social sciences is at least an equally fruitless exercise at the present time.

Hollis: I am unconvinced for a reason I shall presently air. But let us first stake out the ground further. That is your answer for sociology's external boundary. What about within the discipline itself? Does role-theory explain whatever has a sociological explanation? Or do you sometimes need a separate appeal to, for instance, the working of the 'social system'?

Heading: Let me start by pointing out that I have refrained, perhaps pedantically, from talking about role-theory for the obvious reason that I am not convinced that we have, as yet, any role-theory worth boasting about, if we agree to think of theory as a set of interrelated propositions with some empirical support.

I distinguish between possible 'external' and 'internal' role-theory. By the former, which is our main concern in this discussion, I refer to attempts by the role analyst to explain how much and what sort of human action belong to role-theory, by the latter to attempts to develop theories within the role-orientation. Certainly there has been some limited 'internal' development of role-theory addressing itself to questions such as: what explains the different and similar positions and roles found in different societies, organizations and small groups? We should not forget that functionalism originated as an attempt to answer this question; (conflict theorists, however important their contribution to sociological analysis, have not addressed themselves to it systematically). How much role-consensus is there in different social positions and why? What are the consequences for 'society' and individual participants of differing amounts of consensus? What affects the amount of status and role-conflict? What are the mechanisms of conflict resolution? 'External' role-theory has been neglected. Most sociologists have maintained a silence on this subject, a silence which certainly ought to be an embarrassed one since any theory requires some postulates about scope. The reason for the silence is obvious — unwillingness to commit oneself on a subject of professional importance and disagreement. But certain points can and must be made. First, even if all sociology is role-analysis we would not know exactly how much human action it explains for the reasons given above. But secondly, many users of the role-approach believe that certain types of 'social' behaviour cannot be explained in terms of conformity with norms; indeed one of the main criticisms of the sociology of Talcott Parsons is its almost complete focus upon normative conformity.

At least we should recognize the possibility of observable consequences of acting out roles that are *unanticipated* by present actors and certainly by the original norm-formulators. Examples of such consequences are Weber's suggestion that people upholding the 'Protestant Ethic' were particularly likely to engage in rational, capitalistic behaviour (a form of behaviour not mentioned in the norms and certainly unanticipated and probably undesired by Calvin), and Durkheim's demonstration that people adhering to the norms of different religions have different suicide rates. In addition, some sociologists stress that there is no automatic correlation between norms and individuals' attitudes and behaviour and, hence, behavioural regularities may occur that are at variance with the norms imputed to participants by sociologists. The discrepancy might then be explained by a lack of normative or attitudinal consensus amongst the participants (which itself requires demonstration and explanation) or by differential pressure to dissatisfaction and 'deviation' by people variously located in the society because they are more or less able to fulfil their expectations (usually called 'interests' by conflict theorists who, in my opinion, fail adequately to examine the nature and origin of these 'interests') within the existing distribution of power, authority or economic awards.

This brings us to your question about 'social systems'. A 'system' refers simply to a number of interdependent positions and roles, with 'boundaries', more or less permeable, with the external environment, e.g. a total society conceived of as a social system, an economic system, a university. Within such systems, role-analysis views actors as occupants of positions socialized to hold, and rewarded for holding, certain 'legitimate' goals which they attempt to achieve by legitimate means in interaction with occupants of other positions. But Karl Marx, Robert Merton and many others have demonstrated that not all socially significant action in a given social system can be explained in these terms. The classic Marxian analysis of the working of a capitalist free-market showed that the system operated, in practice, in ways unanticipated by those responsible for its introduction. For example, it limited employers' free choice in how to treat their employees and required them not simply to make a 'satisfactory' profit as an indicator of their social usefulness but one approaching the maximum possible, if they were to introduce the most efficient, cost-reducing techniques, which were essential for survival; it produced inevitably crises of over-production, more correctly seen as due to under-consumption, resulting from the existing distribution of economic rewards; it led equally inevitably to the concentration of capital, the squeezing out of many 'owner-controllers' and the increased inability of intending new capitalists to start production competitively in established industries. None of these results was anticipated in the original norms justifying and regulating the system. The Mertonian analysis of American society suggested, as I mentioned earlier, that the pressure to deviate, and actual deviation, was, and remains, particularly great amongst the lower strata who suffer most in their pursuit of 'success' by legitimate means, from the inequality of opportunity built into the system. In an extension of that analysis, I have suggested that creating near-equality of opportunity is unlikely to reduce crime rates because it does not help overcome, and may increase, the problems associated with the pursuit of the inherently limitless goal of 'success', a situation in which attainments can only be relative rather than absolute and which I described as one of 'institutionalized anomie'. A role analyst might claim that these are simply examples of system 'malintegration', but that neither explains their existence nor diminishes their significance.

There are, therefore, behavioural regularities that are recognized by some sociologists as having great social significance and that are not examined adequately, if at all, within orthodox role-theory.

Hollis: Our original question was whether the self is the sum of its roles; and your answer is now clear. You take it to be a query about the scope and kind of social programming. Sociology explains all and only what is in the social programme; role theory explains all and only what men do out of, so to speak, 'duty'. So it at first looks as if the quirks of the individual personality show that sociology has an external boundary and role-theory an internal one. But you do not yet wish to draw that conclusion. For, biology aside, the individual personality is not a psychologist's monopoly, and psychic quirks may have sociological explanations. So, in recognizing sociologist, psychologist and biologist as a triumvirate, you are leaving open a final and empirical question about their relative importance. If the sociologist turns out to hold the trumps, there will finally be no external boundary. If the role-theorist in particular holds them, then the self is after all the sum of its roles. Is that right?

Heading: That is my position.

Hollis: Then I have two bones to pick. One concerns your notion of explanation and the other your view of which questions are empirical. (Incidentally I am struck that sociologists, who operate at the loftiest levels of metaphysical abstraction, so often meet philosophical doubts by saying that their questions are empirical.) Let us tackle your notion of explanation first.

Your methodology is Positivist. Crucial to it is a notion of scientific law, according to which prediction and explanation are two sides of the same coin.

c

Perhaps you will let me just sketch the position, otherwise my queries about your view will not be clear.

The history of the world, as a Positivist sees it, is the history of a series of particular events which just happen to form patterns. Nothing *must* be as it is, no event *must* have a given cause, no event *must* be followed by any other. There is no knowing *a priori* what will happen next. All our knowledge of the world comes from observation and, as the old tag has it, 'the senses reveal no necessities'. The strongest claim which observation can ever justify is of the form, 'A regularly varies with B in conditions C'.

Science therefore has to be an empirical process of amassing generalizations from experience. When asked why something happened, we can only reply by stating the conditions in which such events are usual. To try to go further and, for instance, to seek the hidden machinery behind the veil of appearances would be to abandon Positivism. Phenomena are the only world and the only connections among them are those of regular correlation in specifiable conditions. To claim more is to go beyond the limits of possible knowledge.

Explanation and prediction are thus a matter of isolating regularities. To predict is to forecast an instance of a regularity; to explain is to find a regularity for an instance. Prediction and explanation are the two sides of the only epistemological coin there is. By this account, human behaviour is amenable to science only if it is predictable in given conditions and biology, psychology and role-theory explain only insofar as they predict.

Heading: Well, that is indeed the standard account, though I see no reason why such an approach employing imaginative hypotheses cannot go some way in seeking, if not discovering, 'the hidden machinery'. In asking whether the self is usefully interpreted as the sum of the individual's roles, we are asking which science, with its distinctive hypotheses, supplies the most powerful generalizations.

Hollis: That is what I dispute. May we revert to the topic of innovation and the 'unscientific' belief that men sometimes act as individuals? Take the case of a chess master who plays 30 Kt–K6 in order to gain positional advantage. Let us assume the move to be neither required nor forbidden by the role of master. In your view that makes his choice of move a matter for psychology (or perhaps biology). But is it? You are bound to hold that the move has a psychological explanation, only if masters regularly play that sort of move from that sort of motive in that sort of position. I find that implausible. Previous cases are neither necessary nor sufficient to explain his move. They are not necessary, since he may not know of them and may have decided after making his own analysis. They are not sufficient, since he has to decide for himself, whether the move was sound on previous occasions. Only a foolish master plays Capablanca's moves *because* Capablanca played them. Besides what counts is a matter for the theory of chess and not for scientific observation. So here is a case where an action is explicable because it is rational but not explicable by the Positivist canons of explanation.

Heading: That is an example of the hypothesis of 'rational man' put forward by some sociologists and most economists. At its most applicable, as in your example, I find it unsatisfactory. Why does the master want to gain positional advantage? Because it is in his role to do so. Why do his attempts to gain a good position involve only certain possible moves? Because the rules of chess, which he accepts, only permit certain types of move. Can the particular move be explained without reference to the situation of the game? Remember that I admitted earlier that the situation of the actor is central to an explanation of a *particular* innovation. I suggest, therefore, that an account of his action is inadequate, or at least uninteresting, without considering his role of chess player and the situation in his game. And I wonder why, in your search for general causes of innovation, you prefer rational to irrational behaviour?

Hollis: But you have already agreed (or at least did not dispute it) that role-analysis explains only what a man is required by his roles to do. If you agree also that some chess moves are neither required nor forbidden by the role of chess master (and you can hardly deny it), then role-analysis does not explain why he plays them. Yet rational moves have rational explanations. The master explains by analysing the position why he played that particular move; the role theorist explains by analysing the role why the master was in general playing to win. The sociological explanation is of the 'general-law' variety and does not explain the particular move; the rational explanation is not of the general variety and does explain the move. (That is why I prefer rational innovation. Irrational behaviour may well fit your model.)

Heading: Whether an action is rational is a matter of the standards by which it is judged. These standards are relative to the culture in which they occur. They are therefore examples of A being correlated with B in conditions C, which, I suppose, implies the restoration of Positivism to supremacy. It is in the master's role to play moves which are rational, by the standards of his culture and given the goals prescribed for him in his role.

Hollis: Well, do you regard a choice among standards of reason as a rational choice? Are there, for instance, good reasons for accepting a Positivist philosophy of science?

Heading: Yes, because it helps to produce better predictions and 'more adequate' explanations than alternative philosophies and hence allows greater understanding of, and control over, the environment. We have been socialized to value these advantages of the Positivist philosophy of science and to appreciate the inadequacies of the alternatives in terms of them. When judging the rationality of an action, we usually attempt to decide whether it is an effective means to a given end, whether 'immediate' or 'ultimate', the former being a means to the latter; I believe that we both regard the issue of whether ends may be chosen rationally as unsettled. In addition, I suppose that we are less interested in whether the actor believes his act to be rational than in the judgment of 'knowledgeable observers'. Now, given the end of effective prediction of certain events and hence of 'understanding' of their cause, I believe that Positivist 'value-free' methods are demonstrably effective means. But we might have been socialized to be uninterested in precise prediction or to have 'higher levels' of understanding and you would surely agree that the application of Positivist methods would not then be rational. Moreover, as I mentioned earlier, any act may have unanticipated consequences, and the consequences of scientific achievement might undermine the attainment of other ends, possibly more highly valued than effective prediction, such as adherence to traditional religious, astrological or political practices, and hence be irrational means to the overall attainment of our ends. Like most sociologists and all scientists, I regard the game of science as, so to speak, objectively rational at the first order but relative at the second. I mean that it is an efficient means to an end, but that there is nothing inevitable or necessarily desirable about holding that particular end.

Hollis: That is both staggeringly ambitious and hopelessly modest. It is ambitious in that it claims that all quarrelling with Positivism is a failure to understand the orthodox and accepted criteria of objective inquiry. Since you cannot prove that claim without blatant circularity, I am free to reject it. But the hopeless modesty of the claim is far more destructive. It leads you to a total and absurd scepticism.

We ask of role-theory, I presume, that it be coherent and compatible with all known facts. The presupposition here, as in all science, is that the criteria of coherence are independent of role-theory and that facts are what they are independent of how we label them. Otherwise any theory is as good as any other.

Heading: Yes, those are the conventions about objectivity which we have been socialized into accepting.

Hollis: If you mean 'conventions' (and you have said you do), then you imply that they are in the end arbitrary or, at least, optional. We do not do by convention what we have a good objective reason for doing. So you imply that we are in principle free to accept whatever we please as coherent and true, except insofar as we are too heavily socialized to change the conventions.

Heading: Don't be ridiculous! I am suggesting that we have been socialized both to value certain types of prediction, explanation, coherence and truth, and to accept certain means to their attainment, because they are objectively effective. The latter are conventions to the extent that every user does not have to rediscover them for himself, but he can justify their use or improve upon them. Your position would suggest that there were no facts, no data for sociological theory and no possibility of theoretical progress!

Hollis: I know it would. But isn't that what your second-order relativity comes to? You cannot be neutral about everything. It is all very well to start by saying, 'Sociology explains norms but does not judge them'. But if you apply the doctrine to the norms of sociology, there ceases to be any reason to prefer one theory to

another except on ground of habit. Sociology cannot possibly explain everything —
if it could, there would be nothing to explain!

Heading: Very well. What has that to do with the chess master?

Hollis: In some cases, at any rate, to show why an action was rational is
sufficiently to explain it. But it is not to explain it by citing one of those covering
laws beloved by Positivists. Consequently, in so far as Positivism defines the
methodology of sociology, psychology and biology, not all significant behaviour
is explicable by those sciences. A human agent is more than a bundle of correlations
between properties in given conditions. You have spoken of the 'individual
personality'; but as if the individual were unique because he just happened to
be the only bundle with his particular selection of law-like properties. In other
words, you have no place for a self which is the sum neither of its roles nor of its
psychological nor of its biological properties. Against this, I maintain that rational
action fits a model of explanation incompatible with yours better than it fits yours;
and that, if this model is ever the right one, then it follows that the self is not the
sum of its roles and not a bundle of psychological or biological properties.

Heading: That sounds very mystical to me! You owe us at least a clearer picture
of your actor. In positing him as 'rational man', you are relying, I reckon, on your
'understanding'. Max Weber would no doubt approve this much, but he would have
required also that any hypotheses you generate be tested by Positivist methods.
How do you define 'rationality'? What indicates its presence or absence in a given
situation? Why have 'rational men' produced, and continue to produce, such very
different societies and institutions? Your claim is cautious — that *in some cases* to
show why an action was rational is sufficient to explain it — and invites the
question: when is 'rational' explanation not enough and why?

Hollis: Those are fair questions but they conceal the point I am after. I am not
pitting hypothesis against hypothesis but theory against theory. Earlier you defined
a theory as 'a set of interrelated propositions with some empirical support'. That is
indeed the Positivist theory of 'theory'. It has to be, because of the crucial Positivist
belief that all significant statements about matters of fact are verifiable or refutable
only by experience. In other words, there is, within Positivism, no final distinction
between theories and hypotheses; a theory is simply a set of hypotheses. Now a
theory in pure mathematics or formal logic, for instance, is not 'a set of interrelated
propositions with some empirical support'. It is an *a priori* structure usually
consisting of a set of axioms and, in principle, all their implications. Its axioms
and theorems do not have what a Positivist regards as 'empirical support' and
success in prediction is not the test of its soundness. What sort of theory, then,
do you take a role-theory to be?

Heading: It aims at being a set of confirmed and co-ordinated laws, i.e.
propositions with great empirical support. However, at present, it is a set of fairly
plausible propositions and more concrete hypotheses awaiting confirmation.

Hollis: I do not believe you! If you are right, the role theorist advances by issuing testable predictions; whereas, it seems to me, the social sciences are not straightforwardly predictive and indeed not, in the Positivist sense, predictive at all. Certainly you do not produce statements of the simple form 'in circumstances C, X will happen', and, if you did, you would have to reject good hypotheses for bad reasons. (The economists' Law of Demand, for instance, does not say 'whenever prices rise, demand falls', but, if it did, it would have to be scrapped at once.) Instead the usual form is, 'In circumstances C, if *ceteris* are *paribus,* X will happen'. Now there is no confirming or refuting a hypothesis, if, from the fact that X fails to happen in circumstances C, it follows logically that *ceteris* were *imparibus.* Yet this seems to me to be standardly the case where the 'hypothesis' (like the Law of Demand) is basic to the theory or discipline.

Heading: So, for role-theory to fit my previous answer, it has to specify its *ceteris paribus* clauses in such a way that whether they are satisfied is independent of the truth of the theory.

Hollis: Yes, and hence your earlier willingness to leave the external and internal boundaries of the theory open aroused my suspicions. If boundaries are open, each science is free to preserve its pet hypotheses against all refutation. Thus the sociologist can blame exceptions on psychological quirks of the 'individual personality'; the psychologist can appeal to interfering social facts.

Heading: I agree that boundary disputes are crucial in the end. But they are unlikely to be resolved in the near future and, meanwhile, we retain the role hypotheses and attempt to use them empirically, while striving to develop adequate tests of their claims. They serve, if only because we lack plausible alternative hypotheses to explain behavioural regularities which interest us.

Hollis: But, without boundaries, you cannot test their claims! Men, you said yourself, do not always do what it is in their role to do. So the predictions of role-analysis are not always fulfilled. But you (rightly) do not hold the failure to refute the analysis, unless *ceteris* are *paribus.* Unless you know independently when *ceteris* are *paribus,* your statements are not, by your own Positivist criteria, hypotheses and your science is not predictive.

Heading: But any theory is surely useless, unless it is predictive?

Hollis: Well, at the very start of our discussion, you put a normative element into the definition of 'role'. This means that you regard role-analysis as telling us not, in the first instance, what men will do but what they ought to do in given situations. Prediction is presumably of what men will do. But, if a man does x, it does not follow that he ought to have done it; nor, if he does not do x, that he ought not. Prediction of when men will do what they should do is at most a sub-division of your enterprise and perhaps belongs wholly to, for example, psychology. The role theorist's primary task, I venture to suggest, is to tell us what roles there are, how they are related, what their content is and the other questions you laid out earlier. It is a highly theoretical task — simply asking the actors is not enough — and a role-theory therefore slices the social world up for us. Indeed it almost creates it, in the sense that the categories which we apply affect the way we perceive social relations.

Heading: That sounds relativistic after all!

Hollis: Not, I hope, if we cease to regard theories as Positivists would have us regard them. For a Positivist, truth always lies in the facts and the rest is mere words, defined as we please. There are no *a priori* truths about the world and so no pure theories which are informative. I see no reason to accept this account. You will recall, for instance, that Durkheim's *Elementary Forms of the Religious Life* starts with a bow to Kant and continues by seeking the essence of 'religion', which Durkheim finds in his distinction between sacred and profane. This whole strategy is quite illicit by the Positivist rubric. For a Positivist, Kant was wrong to look for ultimate categories of the human understanding and definitions can never be 'true' or 'real'. Against this, I suggest that the strategy is perfectly in order (whether or not Durkheim applied it successfully). Role-theory ought to be in the end an *a priori* account of an elementary form of the social life.

Heading: But that would turn the statements of role-theory into pure tautologies and make nonsense of experiment and empirical research, because it allows no possibility of breaking out of the tautology.

Hollis: *De tautologis non disputandum,* you mean. I agree. But I do not accept your Positivist interpretation. Mathematics is just such an exercise in *a priori* theorizing but no one thinks that makes nonsense of engineering. Experiment is like work on a mathematical conjecture. If the mathematician suspects but cannot prove that four colours are enough to colour any map so that no two regions of the same colour touch, then he may start drawing maps to try to conjecture out. When he can prove or disprove it, there is no longer any need for maps. Theorizing is difficult and experiment supplies the *vis negativae instantiae.*

Heading: Well, that does come closer to some sociologists' habits than does the Positivist orthodoxy but I am bound to reject it as an account of science. Such an approach is not particularly enlightening unless it tells us *how much* of social life is explained by role-theory. Earlier, you required me, quite rightly, to say something about the scope of this theory and you now define away the problem of scope by your tautological conception of theory. Any attempt to discover how much of all action is explained by role-analysis requires empirical research, research designed to discover, first, what roles, if any, exist for a given status, secondly the extent to which later behaviour accords with predictions made on the assumption of normative conformity and, thirdly, reasons for different rates of nonconformity.

Of course, hypotheses testing the theory must be set up so that they can be refuted by the evidence. As you recognized earlier, the Theorist faced with negative findings must decide whether to explain them away by claiming that *ceteris* were *imparibus* or whether to re-examine critically the basic proposition of role-theory that behavioural regularities are the result of conforming to shared norms.

Hollis: Then we must agree to differ. But perhaps my reason for picking out rational actions now seems more worthy. I see role-theory as a highly theoretical account of the structure of social duties (what you call normative expectations). To meet the snag that such a theory is self-sustaining and untestable, I propose a mathematical model of explanation. This is an *a priori* and anti-Positivist model but it resembles those linear-programming models in economic theory, which tell us not what men will do but how they could do it better. They are models of rational action and explain only rational action. Similarly role-theory seems to me most promisingly construed as an *a priori* model of 'dutiful action'. If you want to claim more, then 'role' will have to be *the* elementary form of the social life.

4

ROLE AND VALUE DEVELOPMENT
ACROSS THE LIFE-CYCLE[1]

CHAD GORDON

Ralph Turner's excellent integration and extension of role theory[2] provides a comprehensive synthesis of the patterned ways in which role dimensions are interrelated at various interaction, organization and institutional levels. The present author's recently-developed theoretical perspective on the life-cycle is based on the changing role relations and value themes that characterize ten relatively distinct stages, and so it is hoped that combining this temporal perspective with Turner's cultural, structural, and interaction process model will result in a moderately comprehensive approach to role and value development across the individual's life-cycle.

Figure 1 presents the major propositions of Turner's system. Almost all can be seen to have significant explanatory power in relation to the acquisition, modification and relinquishment of roles and the major value themes or objectives that form the organizing core of the role's meanings. However, the primary concern of this paper will center on the implications of the ideas in section A (on emergence and character of roles), section D (on role in various societal settings), and section E (on role and person). The numbers of the propositions will be used in parentheses in connection with particular generalizations concerning the life-cycle as a way of explicitly indicating their particular relevance. While other relevancies will be noted in passing, these major sections hold the greatest potential for understanding the ways in which significant persons in key organizational and institutional contexts socialize the developing individual regarding cognitive and emotional content and culturally-provided value themes, and into particular roles that are connected to, and partly derived from, these value themes. It is through this socio-cognitive socialization process that babies become persons and persons become members.

---

1 This chapter is a substantial adaptation and revised version of a previously unpublished paper entitled 'Socialization across the life-cycle: a stage developmental model' (Harvard University, Department of Social Relations mimeograph, December 1969). The original version dealt more with self-conceptions and gave less emphasis to social roles.

2 R. H. Turner, 'Role: sociological aspects', in D. L. Sills (ed.), *International Encyclopedia of the Social Sciences,* 13 (New York, 1968), pp. 552-7.

Figure 1: Turner's system of role theory propositions [adapted from Ralph H. Turner, *Role: Sociological Aspects* (1968)]

A. EMERGENCE AND CHARACTER OF ROLES

1. *Role differentiation and accretion:*

   In any interactive situation, behavior, sentiments, and motives tend to be differentiated into units, which can be called roles; once roles are differentiated, elements of behavior, sentiment, and motives which appear in the same situation tend to be assigned to the existing roles.

2. *Meaningfulness:*

   In any interactive situation, the meaning of individual actions for ego (the actor) and for any alters is assigned on the basis of the imputed role.

3. *Role cues:*

   In connection with every role there is a tendency for certain aspects of behavior, typical situation, and typical attributes of the actor to become salient as cues to role identification.

4. *Behavioral correspondence:*

   There is a tendency for the character of a role to shift toward correspondence with the consistent patterns of behavior that are observed in the context of these roles.

5. *Evaluation:*

   Every role tends to acquire an evaluation, both in terms of rank and in terms of its socially favorable or detrimental character.

B. ROLE AS INTERACTIVE FRAMEWORK

6. *Interaction:*

   The establishment and persistence of interaction tends to depend upon the emergence and identification of ego and alter roles.

7. *Role complementarity:*

   Each role tends to form as a comprehensive way of coping with one or more relevant alter roles.
   Corollary, 7a: The adaptiveness of any item of behavior or other role component in dealing with the alter role is subordinated to its place in the total role as an adaptive strategy.

8. *Role consensus:*

   There is a tendency toward consensus regarding the content of roles in interaction; however, the degree of consensus required for a viable interactive system is not great.

9. *Legitimate expectation:*

There is a tendency for stabilized roles to be assigned the character of legitimate expectations.

Corollary, 9a: To the extent to which the selection of ego's role (and to a lesser degree the enactment of his role) depend upon alter's selection of role or performance of parts of the role, ego will convert his expectations into legitimate expectations regarding alter's role.

Corollary, 9b: To the extent to which alter's role is positively valued, with respect to rank and favorableness, ego will translate his anticipations regarding alter's role into legitimate expectations.

10. *Role persistence:*

Once stabilized, the role structure tends to persist, regardless of changes in the actors.

Corollary, 10a: When an actor leaves the group and is replaced by another, there is a tendency to allocate to him the role played by the former member.

Corollary, 10b: If one actor changes roles, there is a tendency for another actor to make a compensatory change of roles so as to maintain the original role structure.

11. *Role allocation:*

There is a tendency to identify a given individual with a given role, and a complementary tendency for an individual to adopt a given role, for the duration of the interaction.

12. *Role-taking:*

To the extent to which ego's role is an adaptation to alter's role, it incorporates some conception of alter's role.

13. *Role adequacy:*

Role behavior tends to be judged as adequate or inadequate by comparison with a conception of the role in question.

Corollary, 13a: To the degree to which a role is favorably evaluated, judgments of role adequacy tend to be translated into evaluations of the person playing the role.

14. *Role reciprocity:*

The degree of role adequacy legitimately expected of ego tends to be a function of the degree of role adequacy attributed to alter.

Corollary, 14a: The degree to which ego can legitimately claim the privileges of his role tends to be a function of his degree of role adequacy.

Corollary, 14b: Since role behavior does not normally correspond precisely with the role conceptions, legitimate expectations are adjusted in the course of interaction in response to either over-adequacy or under-adequacy.

C. ROLE IN AN ORGANIZATIONAL SETTING

15. *Organizational goal dominance:*

    To the extent to which roles are incorporated into an organizational setting, organizational goals tend to become the crucial criteria for role differentiation, evaluation, complementarity, legitimacy of expectation, consensus, allocation and judgments of adequacy.

16. *Legitimate role definers:*

    To the extent to which roles are incorporated into an organizational setting, the right to define the legitimate character of roles, to set the evaluations on roles, to allocate roles, and to judge role adequacy tend to be lodged in particular roles.

17. *Status:*

    To the extent to which roles are incorporated into an organizational setting, differentiation tends to link roles to statuses in the organization.

18. *Role-set:*

    To the extent to which roles are incorporated into an organizational setting, each role tends to develop as a pattern of adaptation to multiple alter roles.

19. *Formalization:*

    To the extent to which roles are incorporated into an organizational setting, the persistence of roles is intensified through tradition and formalization.

D. ROLE IN A SOCIETAL SETTING

20. *Economy of roles:*

    Similar roles in different contexts tend to become merged, so as to be identified as a single role recurring in different relationships.
    Corollary, 20a: Roles in situations of limited generality and social significance tend to be shaped in accordance with the pattern of roles in situations of greater generality and social significance.

21. *Value anchorage:*

    To the extent to which roles are referred to a societal context, differentiation tends to link roles to social values; status [organizational position] is not diminished as a point of anchorage, but social values take the place of organizational goals as major anchorages for roles.

22. *Allocation consistency:*

    The individual in society tends to be assigned and to assume roles which are consistent with one another.
    Corollary, 22a: Roles that have greatest generality tend to serve as qualifying criteria for allocation of other roles; age, sex, and socioeconomic status tend to be key roles in this sense.

E. ROLE AND PERSON

23. *Role strain:*

The actor tends to act so as to alleviate role strain arising out of role contradiction, role conflict, and role inadequacy, and to heighten the gratifications of high role adequacy.

24. *Socialization:*

The individual in society tends to adopt as a framework for his own behavior and as a perspective for the interpretation of the behavior of others a repertoire of role relationships. Thus socialization is partly a matter of learning somewhat culturally standard role conceptions and partly a matter of learning to constitute the social world through enactment of role processes with their tentative and adaptive character.

25. *Self-conception:*

The individual tends to form a self-conception [in part] by selective identification of certain roles from his repertoire as more characteristically 'himself' than other roles.

Corollary, 25a: *Self-evaluation* — The self-conception takes on also the evaluative aspects of the roles which are incorporated into the self-conception. On the basis of the roles included, the individual is said to develop *a sense of personal prestige* . . . on the basis of his perceptions of role *adequacy* in these most 'ego-involved' roles, the individual develops a *self-esteem*. To some degree these two forms of self-evaluation are kept separate, but to a considerable degree they are combined into a more *generalized self-estimate*.

Corollary, 25b: *Adaptivity of self-conception* — The self-conception tends to stress those roles which supply the basis for effective adaptation to relevant alters.

26. *Role distance:*

To the extent to which roles which must be played in situations contradict the self-conception, these roles will be assigned role distance, and mechanisms of demonstrating lack of personal involvement will be employed.

A SOCIO-COGNITIVE STAGE MODEL OF ROLE AND VALUE DEVELOPMENT ACROSS THE LIFE-CYCLE

Figure 2 presents the ten life-cycle stages being proposed,[1] showing the most significant other persons involved in the socialization process, the major dilemma of value-theme differentiation and integration at each stage, and the approximate ages that each stage spans in contemporary, urban, middle-class America (or at least those portions not yet dramatically affected by the 'counter culture'[2] or Consciousness III[3]).

---

[1] C. Gordon, 'Socialization across the life-cycle: A stage-developmental model', Harvard University, Department of Social Relations mimeograph.

[2] T. Roszak, *The Making of a Counter Culture: Reflections on the Technocratic Society and its Youthful Opposition* (Garden City, N.Y., 1969).

[3] C. A. Reich, *The Greening of America* (New York, 1970).

Figure 2: Stage developmental model of the ideal–typical life-cycle in contemporary, urban, middle-class America — giving approximate ages, the most significant other persons, and the major dilemmas of value-theme differentiation and integration

Life-cycle stage	Approximate ages	Most significant others	Major dilemma of value-theme differentiation and integration security/challenge
I. Infancy	0–12 months	mother	Affective gratification/ sensorimotor experiencing
II. Early childhood	1–2 years	mother, father	Compliance/self-control
III. Oedipal period	3–5 years	father, mother, siblings, play-mates	Expressivity/ instrumentality
IV. Later childhood	6–11 years	parents, same sex peers, teachers	Peer relationships/ evaluated abilities
V. Early adolescence	12–15 years	parents, same sex peers, opposite sex peers, teachers	Acceptance/achievement
VI. Later adolescence	16–20 years	same sex peers, opposite sex peers, parents, teachers, loved one, wife or husband	Intimacy/autonomy
VII. Young adulthood	21–29 years	loved one, husband, or wife, children, employers, friends	Connection/self-determination
VIII. Early maturity	30–44 years	wife or husband, children, superiors, colleagues, friends, parents	Stability/ accomplishment
IX. Full maturity	45 to retirement age	wife or husband, children, colleagues, friends, younger associates	Dignity/control
X. Old age	Retirement age to death	remaining family, long-term friends, neighbours	Meaningful integration/autonomy

Any new theory of the life-cycle must by necessity and desire draw heavily upon three major contributors to analysis of human development. Erik Erikson[1] first transformed the Freudian psychoanalytic perspective on the relations of the child and his parents into a more extended drama, focusing on the interplay of social roles and personality dynamics. Talcott Parsons[2] incorporated the psychoanalytic stages of psychosexual development into his general theory of action by showing how the fundamental analytic dimensions of all action systems apply to the family, the parent—child interactions and to the child's developing personality. He suggested that these basic dimensions structure the differentiation and integration of the child's motivational dispositions, values, and role orientations. Most recently, Theodor Lidz, a psychiatrist with long experience concerning family determinants of schizophrenia, published a masterly and brilliant book with the title *The Person: His Development Through the Life Cycle*[3] that again recasts the genuine insights of the psychoanalytic perspective, but this time in connection with the entire range of persons significant to the developing individual, into even the most advanced years.

These works of Erikson, Parsons and Lidz have been used as basic background orientation for the present analysis, and will be quoted extensively for their essential insights. The present model, however, differs from these antecedent works in that it tries to provide a consistent, comprehensive and systematic formulation of the crucial dilemmas of *value-theme differentiation and integration* that are produced by the interaction of physical maturation, cognitive elaboration and role alterations. It is these interactions and dilemmas that structure the changing stages in the socio-cognitive development during a human life-cycle.

'Value-theme' in this context means a cluster or complex of culturally defined and idealized aspects of human life and social interaction, such as achievement, acceptance, compliance, self-control, and the like. These very general motivational complexes or value orientations are simultaneously *institutionalized* in a social system's culture and social structure and *internalized* as constitutive components of individual personalities of the social system's members. Socialization is just this process, whereby institutionalized value-themes become internalized *in some version* in the personality and self-conceptions of most, if not all, of the social system's members.

An assumption of this approach is that the value-themes are so general and so solidly built into the role relationships of socialization that every person being

---

1   E. H. Erikson, 'Growth and crises of the healthy personality', in E. H. Erikson (ed.), *Identity and the Life Cycle (Psychological Issues, vol. I, no. 1, 1950)*, pp. 50-100. E. H. Erikson, 'The problem of ego identity', *Journal of the American Psychoanalytic Association,* 4 (1956), 56-121.
2   T. Parsons, 'The American family: its relations to personality and to the social structure', pp. 3-33; 'Family structure and the socialization of the child', pp. 35-131; 'The organization of personality as a system of action', pp. 133-86, in T. Parsons and R. F. Bales, *Family: Socialization and Interaction Process* (Glencoe, Ill., 1955).
3   T. Lidz, *The Person: His Development through the Life Cycle* (New York, 1968).

socialized at one of the particular stages must in some fashion come to terms with the value-symbolism and motivational orientations at issue.

These culturally patterned symbolic meanings and major value-orientations are taken to establish a set of very significant dimensions of differentiation and integration at each stage in the life cycle. The model is formulated on the basic theory that a relatively small number of reasonably distinct combinations of physical maturation, cognitive elaboration and role relationships with agents of socialization establish a particular context in which a certain pair of value-themes emerge from the culture of the socializers. These are made directly relevant and inescapable to the person being socialized.

Five orienting assumptions should be stated explicitly at the outset. First, while it is quite obvious that many other elements are also being made relevant in the interaction between socializer and socializee, it is argued that certain pairs of general value-themes are held by quite diverse cultures to be essential elements of socialization at the indicated stages, even though degrees of emphasis will surely differ between cultures and sub-cultures.[1] The discussion will focus on contemporary, middle-class, urban America. Second, these value-theme pairs are here interpreted as closely connected with the interactions and resolutions of socialization in the previous stage. Third, it is argued that these value-theme pairs pose a problem of integration for the socializee in that they are to a degree mutually inconsistent. The dilemma can be integrated or resolved only through a temporarily stable balance or equilibrium, which can and will be disrupted by continual restructuring and recombining of physical maturation, cognitive elaboration and social role relations. Fourth, it is asserted (although not documented in this limited space) that a structurally equivalent social process (involving in order the elements of permissiveness, support, denial of reciprocity and manipulation of rewards) is the mechanism that at each stage produces the new socialized learning and resolution. This then remains relatively stable until it is disrupted by significant changes in body, cognition or role relations.[2] Fifth, all of the value-theme complexes suggested in this paper are at this point merely hypothetical constructs adduced from fairly extensive theory, very limited research, and assorted fragments of personal experience. Only substantial and solid research can assess their validity and importance.

Figure 3 portrays the proposed life-cycle stages in terms of two major dimensions. The horizontal axis represents the age at which relatively distinct symbolic points of discontinuity tend to occur in the life-cycles of urban, middle-class Americans being socialized in 'normatively prescribed' families where a mother, a father, and one or

1   Cf. R. Benedict, *Patterns of Culture* (Boston, 1934); M. Mead, 'Age patterning in personality development', in D. G. Haring (ed.), *Personal Character and Cultural Milieu,* rev. ed. (Syracuse, N.Y., 1949), pp. 539-48; D. Riesman, N. Glazer, R. Denney, *The Lonely Crowd: A Study of the Changing American Character* (Garden City, N.Y., 1950); F. Kluckhohn and F. L. Strodtbeck, *Variations in Value Orientations* (Evanston, Ill., 1961).
2   T. Parsons, 'Family structure and the socialization of the child', pp. 59ff.

Figure 3: Assumed level of independence of action during each stage of the life-cycle

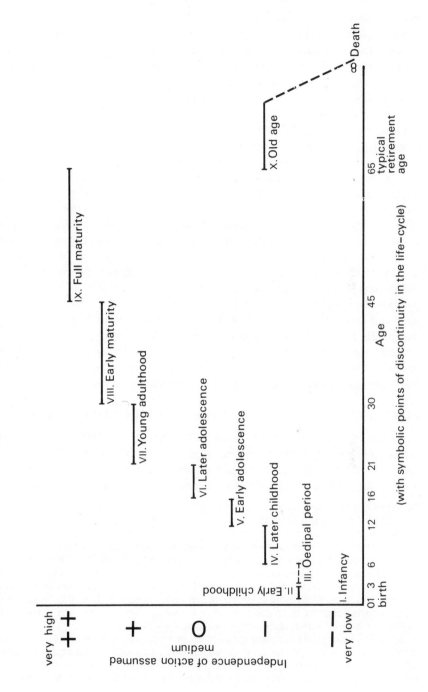

more young children are present in the home. The vertical axis represents (in an intuitive, graphic manner) the level of independence of action assumed by the present theory to characterize personal conduct and role performance at each of the various stages. In this context, socialization is seen as preparing the developing person to utilize ever-expanding capacities and resources in activity patterns that are increasingly self-directed, from infancy through full maturity. Old age very typically brings major reductions in both roles and resources, and is therefore considered as a period of declining independence of action, with the period before death having many similarities to childhood and even infancy.

The rapid succession and accelerating independence of the stages up through age 21 underscore the importance of early socialization in preparing persons for these dramatic developments, while the much greater length of the later stages emphasizes the need for solid theory and research on the relatively neglected later 70 per cent of the life span. Specification of particular age points and graphic discontinuity of the stage representations in Figure 3 are intentionally employed to emphasize the assertion that (in contemporary, middle-class, urban America) a set of biological, cognitive, interactional, social-role, reference-group, organizational and cultural factors tend to cohere to produce relatively distinct changes at or around these points in the life-cycle. The reader should be cautioned one last time to bear in mind that other cultural, social-class, family-structure or occupational configurations may produce appreciable modifications in the timing, value-theme content, transitions and even the discernible existence of the various stages discussed below. Analysis of the principles governing the symbolic transitions between stages, their timing, and relative ease or difficulty must be reserved for a future paper.

CONCEPTUALIZATION OF ROLE USED IN THIS CHAPTER

Regardless of stage, *a role is conceptualized as a pattern of behavior and sentiment, organized in relation to presumed motivations, and frequently but not always connected to a specific organizational position.* This usage is intended to embody Turner's formulation of role, one of the clearest and most fruitful in the field:

By *role* we mean a collection of patterns of behavior which are thought to constitute a meaningful unit and deemed appropriate to a person occupying a particular status in society (e.g., doctor or father), occupying an informally defined position in interpersonal relations (e.g., leader or compromiser), or identified with a particular value in society (e.g., honest man or patriot). We shall stress the point that a role consists of behaviors which are regarded as making up a meaningful unit. The linkage of behaviors within roles is the source of our expectations that certain kinds of action will be found together. When people speak of trying to 'make sense' of someone's behavior or to understand its meaning, they are typically attempting to find the role of which the observed actions are a part.

Role will be consistently distinguished from status or position or value type as referring to the whole of the behavior which is felt to belong intrinsically to those subdivisions. Role refers to behavior rather than position, so that one may *enact* a role but cannot *occupy* a role. However, role is a normative concept. It refers to expected or appropriate behavior and is distinguished from the manner in which the role is actually enacted in a specific situation, which is *role behavior* or *role performance*. While a norm is a directive to action, a role is a *set of norms,* with the additional normative element that the individual is expected to be consistent. The role is made up of all those norms which are thought to apply to a person occupying a given position. Thus, we return to our initial emphasis that the crucial feature of the concept of role is its reference to the assumption that certain different norms are meaningfully related or 'go together'.[1]

The concrete interpretations of role change and value-theme dilemmas associated with each stage in this ideal—typical socio-cognitive model of the life-cycle can perhaps best be communicated by a systematic presentation of the stage's maturational, cognitive, social structural and cultural aspects in serial order. The underlying dimensions of *security* versus *challenge* and the increasing (and ultimately decreasing) level of *independence of action* can then be articulated as leitmotifs in the counterpoint of human development.

Stage I: INFANCY — the first year of life — AFFECTIVE GRATIFICATION AND SENSORIMOTOR EXPERIENCING THROUGH RECEPTIVE AND ACTIVE INCORPORATION

THE FIRST INTERACTIVE ROLE: MY BABY; MY DEPENDENT NEEDER

The new-born child is completely helpless, and totally dependent upon those around him for protection and provision of everything necessary to sustain his life. The shift from reception of all nutrition through the placenta and umbilical cord to suckling of milk through the lips and mouth has led many analysts to consider birth as the 'oral crisis' and infancy as the stage of oral dependency. There is much truth in this view, since the transition to the mouth as the primary organ of transaction with the surrounding environment forms one of the clearest discontinuities in the human life-cycle, since the sucking reflex is an automatic or predetermined pattern, and since so many of the neonate's waking moments are spent in nursing. Yet many other forms of interaction with the social and physical environment are important even at birth, and it seems wiser to consider the more general and essential feature of the first year of life to be the incorporation of stimuli (both physical and symbolic) from the environment. An analysis stemming from this view will examine ways in which this incorporative mode is socially patterned.

Receptive incorporative sub-stage: the first six months

The infant receives much more than just milk, as he is cradled, cuddled, stroked and sung to; he is the recipient of an extraordinarily complex set of stimuli concerning what adults interpret as a mixture of maternal warmth, love, satisfaction and

1   R. H. Turner, 'Role-taking, role standpoint, and reference group behavior', *American Journal of Sociology,* 61 (Jan. 1956), 316-17.

pleasure, as well as maternal rejection, coldness, ambivalence, anxiety, exhaustion, and the like. Although it is not possible to conclude that the infant interprets these stimuli in any direct fashion, the cues are so global and pervasive on the infants' senses that their effects are in all likelihood of strong significance. Observation of these very young infants as they are fed, held, talked to and admired by their mothers and other persons makes it quite clear that incorporation includes much more than mere physical nutrition.

Two major symbolic dimensions characterize even the youngest infant's interaction with his social and physical world: affective gratification and sensorimotor experiencing.

Affective gratification comes to the infant from the manner in which maternal care and nurturance is provided at least as much as from the actual content of that care. Thus two mothers may provide objectively similar kinds of nutrition, cleanliness and protection, yet the affective styles with which this care is provided may convey the warmest cherishing love in one case and the coldest resentful rejection in the other. Research on the relevant dimensions, the mechanisms by which differences in affective orientation are conveyed, and their effects on infants is still inconclusive (see the wide-ranging review by Caldwell),[1] but the *overall* domain of affective gratification seems undeniably fundamental to all later socialization.

Sensorimotor experiencing begins well before birth but even while the infant is predominantly receptive (rather than exploratory, in that he cannot yet crawl about or grasp objects), he is incorporating the environment. That is, he is 'drinking in' visual stimuli (especially faces), listening to the whole range of sounds in the home, smelling and tasting, and finally physically touching and moving all kinds of objects within his small reach. Piaget and his associates have given extensive consideration to the developments of the first six or eight months of life, which are seen as including the first three stages of the sensorimotor period (0-2 years).[2] Incorporation during the first month is comprised of exercising the 'readymade' sensorimotor schemata or 'reflexes'. It involves orienting to light or sound, grasping objects, sucking when the lips or cheeks are touched, vocalizing and waving, etc. Through the fourth month the infant learns to coordinate several of these schemata, to look at and reach for the same object, or listen and look at the same source. Through the eighth month the infant develops the capacity to recognize and center on objects, and to use them with apparent intention to produce an outcome, establishing a means-to-ends relation. This stage is exemplified by such actions as 'shaking the rattle to hear the noise'. Many processes of acquiring cognitive structures by assimilating new materials and accommodating previously acquired

1   B. M. Caldwell, 'The effects of infant care', in M. L. and L. W. Hoffman, *Review of Child Development* (New York, 1964), vol. I, pp. 9-87.
2   J. H. Flavell, *The Developmental Psychology of Jean Piaget* (Princeton, N.J., 1963), ch. 3; J. L. Phillips Jr, *The Origins of Intellect: Piaget's Theory* (San Francisco, 1969), ch. 2.

structures have been explored,[1] but much remains to be learned about the ways in which differences in culture and social structure affect the content and timing of the universal processes. Regardless of culture, the persons caring for the totally helpless infant must define him as a dependent needer, and thus come to define themselves reciprocally as care-givers and controllers (12, 18).

Active incorporative sub-stage: 7–12 months

The nature of sensorimotor experiencing changes as the infant becomes able to roll over, sit up, crawl, stand, and eventually to toddle from place to place with the support of tables, chairs and adult hands. He now *explores* his environment, reaching for every available object and putting it immediately into his mouth. For Piaget, this is the period of coordinating the more elaborate schemata, and especially for much greater attention to the relation of means to ends. This allows simple motor acts to take on symbolic meanings, as in the forms of play and problem-solving, or as representing other actions: in one observation, 'At age eleven months, fifteen days, Jacqueline cries as soon as her mother puts her hat on'. Language learning now goes forward rapidly, even before actual speech by the infant.[2] In all these instances the infant is still incorporating complex structures of both cognitive and affective components, but now he is much more actively seeking out new experiences and is actively producing desired responses in his physical and social worlds. The infant is now able to express both aggressive and loving feelings. In a very real sense the infant's self-initiated actions towards desired incorporations have become the primary element in his interaction with his mother; as Harriet Rheingold has argued in a trenchant paper entitled 'The social and socializing infant', the very small infant uses crying and smiling and his own learning to sanction his parents; 'He teaches them what he needs to have them do for him. He makes them behave in a nurturing fashion; (13, 14) . . . of men and women he makes fathers and mothers.'[3]

This second sub-stage of infancy is one of active rather than passive incorporation in another sense: 'oral aggression', long recognized by those informed by the psychoanalytic perspective, now combines with the pressure of other activities to alter the relation of the mother from one of unceasing nurturance to conditional and intermittent attention.[4] As the infant develops teeth and begins to bite the

[1] J. H. Flavell, *Psychology of Jean Piaget*; J. S. Bruner, R. R. Oliver, P. M. Greenfield *et al.*, *Studies in Cognitive Growth* (New York, 1966); J. L. Gewirtz, 'Mechanisms of social learning: some roles of stimulation and behavior in early human development', in D. Goslin (ed.), *Handbook of Socialization Theory and Research* (New York, 1969).
[2] R. Brown, *Social Psychology* (New York, 1965), chs. 5 and 6; A. R. Jensen, 'Social class and verbal learning', in M. Deutsch, I. Katz and A. R. Jensen, *Social Class, Race, and Psychological Development* (New York, 1968).
[3] H. L. Rheingold, 'The social and socializing infant', in D. Goslin (ed.), *Socialization Theory*, p. 783.
[4] E. H. Erikson, 'Growth and crises of the healthy personality', pp. 59-61; T. Parsons, 'Family structure and the socialization of the child', pp. 62-7; T. Lidz, *The Person*, p. 151.

mother's nipples and fingers, the tenor of her orientation toward him shifts, in what Parsons has formulated as a sequence, from general permissiveness, to denial of reciprocity, to manipulation of positive rewards as the child learns to modulate his dependency demands. This sequence is postulated by Parsons[1] as the basis for the child's internalization of a complex cognitive and affective meaning-structure representing the entire mother—child dependency attachment or relationship. This same sequence is what Freud termed the ego's primary identification.[2] It should be noted that both the theoretical and empirical validity of the concept of identification are matters of substantial dispute.[3] However, those who have been the object of such attachments or observed them closely will attest to the strength and importance of these interpersonal bonds (9).

EARLY ROLE ACQUISITION – THE ROLE OF IMITATIVE LEARNER, AND THE GENDER ROLE: BOY; GIRL

Many sociological treatments of socialization stress the importance of role acquisition, and although this emphasis tends to miss the significance of other socially patterned cognitive and affective learning, the focus on roles can be very productive. During infancy, the role of imitative learner is a very important developmental step beyond the earlier quasi-role 'dependent needer'.[4] Gender-role development also clearly begins during the infancy stage, since even very young infants tend to be treated in rather different fashion depending on their sex (24, 25, 22a).

The major factor at this stage is the social process of labelling. Even before the child's birth, a gender-related name has usually been selected for him, blankets or nursery decorations of particular colors and emblems may have been arranged for him, and he will forever be the target of particular linguistic forms denoting his gender: 'Look how big he's getting; such a strong boy we have!' Although there is now a substantial body of research on early gender-role acquisition,[5] much remains to be learned about the way this and other roles shape self-conceptions and conduct choices.

Throughout the life-cycle, different material and symbolic media are the coinages through which the varying socialization processes are transacted. Early in the infancy period a key generalization is made whereby oral eroticism shifts from merely a material pleasure into a symbolic meaning. As Parsons puts it:

1 T. Parsons, 'Family structure and the socialization of the child', p. 65.
2 S. Freud, *The Ego and the Id* (New York, 1927), p. 31.
3 J. L. Gewirtz, 'Mechanisms of Social Learning', pp. 153-61; A. Bandura, 'Social-learning theory of identificatory processes', in D. Goslin (ed.), *Socialization Theory*.
4 Cf. A. Bandura and R. H. Walters, *Social Learning and Personality Development* (New York, 1963).
5 P. H. Mussen, 'Early sex-role development', in D. Goslin (ed.), *Socialization Theory*; J. Kagan, 'Acquisition and significance of sex typing and sex role identity', in M. L. and L. W. Hoffman (eds.), *Child Development*, vol. 1, pp. 137-68.

There seems no reason to doubt that erotic pleasure has a certain organic specificity. But we believe that the primary significance of eroticism for the socialization process is not that it is one more specific source of gratification like most of the organic needs, but that it has a special significance as a vehicle of generalization . . . Oral gratification, which is necessarily associated with the agent of care by virtue of the critical significance of feeding, can thus come to symbolize the positive aspect of dependency and hence of identification.[1]

It is this symbolic character of oral gratification that allows Parsons, Erikson and others to posit that oral deprivation in infancy, mother's resentment during feeding, abrupt or anxious attempts at weaning, etc., may lead to pessimism, pervasive mistrust or one of the compulsive neuroses in later life, while 'over-gratification' may produce a 'spoiled' or even 'psychopathic' personality configuration.[2] While this perspective has guided the studies collected in a fair amount of research in the culture and personality tradition,[3] the evidence supporting such hypotheses is not very persuasive.

In any case, the communicative interaction between parent and infant always includes both affective and cognitive dimensions, however they may be grounded in generalized or specific organic gratifications. In addition to specific and segmental elements of care and attention, the infant receives diffuse love and gives in return the smiles and vocalizations of affection, mixed with the crying, screaming, kicking and hitting that signify frustration and rage. In addition to his demands for nurturance, his attempts at exploration elicit a range of responses from those watching over him. From these responses he learns that his own action produces results in the external world, and something of the affect with which these responses are associated (25a). On these grounds, it may be speculated that the early experiences of loving acceptance or its opposites may begin to form a diffuse sense of *unity* or solidarity with the parent, and that the parent's responses (or relative paucity of them) will establish the foundations for a sense of *self-determination*. It will be argued here that these and the other major self-conceptions are crucial aspects of socialization and conduct throughout the entire life-cycle.[4]

In addition, the particular nature of the parental responses and reward levels during the first year of life may establish the initial foundations for the child's general coping style, in terms of the dimensions *optimism* v. *pessimism* and *activity* v. *passivity*. The child's degree of optimism regarding the level of future rewards from the social environment is at the heart of Erikson's discussion of 'basic trust' as one of the key developmental attainments of infancy,[5] and the establish-

---

1 T. Parsons, 'Family structure and the socialization of the child', p. 66.
2 T. Parsons and J. Olds, 'The mechanisms of personality functioning with special reference to socialization', in T. Parsons and R. F. Bales, *Family*, pp. 254-6.
3 Cf. C. Kluckhohn and H. A. Murray (eds.), *Personality in Nature, Society, and Culture* (New York, 1959).
4 C. Gordon, 'Systemic senses of self', *Sociological Inquiry,* 38 (Spring), 161-78.
5 E. H. Erikson, 'Growth and crises of the healthy personality', pp. 55-65.

ment of some balance of activity and passivity as a consistent style of interacting with others is the core of the long program of research conducted by Charlotte Bühler and her associates.[1]

In the view presented here, infancy represents a stage in the life-cycle characterized by the interplay between affective gratification and sensorimotor experiencing. The primary relationship is with the mother, with the infant usually being cast into the very broad roles of loved object (baby), dependent needer, imitative learner, and boy or girl. The themes of gratification and learning to a large degree involve alternative activities, and they are complementary in that the early forms of learning seem to be inherently gratifying, and the basic gratifications provide the reinforcement component in the classical learning paradigm. Yet there is also frequent contradiction and paradox between the two. Many of the actively incorporative infant's experiencing attempts will provoke punishments from the parent, and prolonged attachment to the basic gratifications of sleeping, eating and being cuddled can interfere with more instrumental cognitive learning (23).

The pattern of balance between gratification and experiencing does work out in a given case. The position argued here is that the overall interaction between mother and child in the first year of life typically results in some form of parent–child identification, establishment of a well reinforced dependency relation, the beginnings of language learning, initial formation of the child's coping style along the optimism–pessimism and activity–passivity dimensions, and the beginnings of self-conceptions concerning levels of sensed unity and self-determination. Together, these elements form the basis on which the socialization processes continue to work in the next stage, early childhood.

Stage II: EARLY CHILDHOOD – age 1–2 years – COMPLIANCE/SELF CONTROL

Near the close of the first year of life, enough physical maturation has occurred to permit a wide range of control over the major and minor muscle groups. Shortly after his first birthday, the child will be able to walk fairly steadily and soon will be running with confident balance; development of the arm and hand coordination systems allow him to get into nearly anything. Of particular importance to the socialization process are two additional developments around the first birthday: the vocal equipment is now capable of clear pronunciation of single words and word clusters, and the sphincter muscles come under enough control to permit some voluntary delay of bowel and bladder elimination. In the interests of the safety of the walking, talking and investigating toddler, and as an attempt to avoid the unpleasantness of having to clean up after him, the child's parents are very likely to begin to set limits on his behavior and to try to teach him to take care of his own toilet needs. At the same time they are likely to focus on teaching him to under-

1   C. Bühler and F. Massarik (eds.), *The Course of Human Life: a Study of Goals in the Humanistic Perspective* (New York, 1968).

stand and originate speech. These parental expectations and socialization efforts structure the twin emphases of the 1–2 year old period: compliance and self-control.

On the cognitive side, the early childhood holds very great development, encompassing Piaget's stage 5 (12–18 months; development of early concepts of object-permanence, space, time-causality, and the elaboration of means toward desired ends) and stage 6 (18–24 months; development of intentionality and prominence of play and imitation).[1] These capacities for imitating models and for accepting verbal instructions are particularly important for the child's relations with his father; the 'others' of role theory thus become more differentiated (15–19).

The literature on this phase of child development is now very extensive, and rather thoroughly documents the interlinking of compliance and self-control in the sense that the mother and father set up and communicate expectations that the child should imitate their models and comply with their instructions aimed at teaching him to take care of himself in these central areas.[2] Specific patterns and contrasts between differing cultures, social classes, ethnic groups and time periods may be found in Bronfenbrenner.[3]

Yet there is an inherent contradiction or dilemma in the duality of compliance with specific parental demands and self-control over a diffuse set of possible behaviors, as can be seen more clearly when examining the affective aspects of development during the early childhood period. Lidz has framed the problem with poignant clarity:

The dangers, as always, lie on both sides. He cannot yet really be responsible for himself, and he is far from independent. Indeed, his venturesomeness depends upon his having close at hand the shelter of his mother's arms and lap to which he can retreat when he overreaches himself. A mother who finds too anxiety-provoking those activities of her child that lead him into a world full of very real dangers — stairways, gas-vents, lamps that topple, car-filled streets — may overly limit the child, surrounding him with gates, fences, and a barrier of 'no's' that stifle initiative

1 J. H. Flavell, *Psychology of Jean Piaget.*
2 M. L. and L. W. Hoffman (eds.), *Child Development,* vol. 1 and vol. 2; A. Bandura and R. H. Walters, *Social Learning*; P. H. Mussen, J. J. Conger and J. Kagan (eds.), *Readings in Child Development and Personality* (New York, 1965); R. D. Parke (ed.), *Readings in Social Development* (New York, 1969); L. Kohlberg, 'Stage and sequence: the cognitive–developmental approach to socialization', in D. Goslin (ed.), *Socialization Theory,* pp. 347-480; B. R. McCandless, 'Childhood socialization', in D. Goslin (ed.), *Socialization Theory,* pp. 791-819.
3 U. Bronfenbrenner, 'Socialization and social class through time and space', in E. E. Maccoby, T. M. Newcomb and E. L. Hartley (eds.), *Readings in Social Psychology,* 3rd ed. (New York, 1958); see also F. Elkin, *The Child and Society: The Process of Socialization* (New York, 1960); N. W. Bell and E. F. Vogel (eds.), *A Modern Introduction to the Family* (Glencoe, Ill., 1960); W. N. Stephens, *The Family in Cross-cultural Perspective* (New York, 1963); R. F. Winch, *The Modern Family* (New York, 1963); W. J. Goode, *The Family* (Englewood Cliffs, N.J., 1964); S. Coopersmith, *The Antecedents of Self Esteem* (San Francisco, 1967); G. Handel (ed.), *The Psychosocial interior of the Family* (Chicago, 1967); R. F. Winch, and L. W. Goodman (eds.), *Selected Studies in Marriage and the Family,* 3rd ed. (New York, 1968).

and self-confidence. Mothers who have little confidence in their ability to guide and control the child are apt to project such feelings and magnify the child's incapacity to care for himself. Mothers who cannot tolerate disorder, or who over-estimate the baby's capacities to conform and regulate his impulses, can convey a sense of his 'being bad' to the child, and thereby provoke a sense of guilt or shame that undermines his feelings of worth and self-trust. The child may be led into an overconformity that satisfies the parents but covers hostile resistance and stubbornness.[1]

This insightful portrayal of the central dilemma of early childhood highlights three particularly important dimensions of self-conception that are likely to be shaped by the parents' interactions with the child (25b). First, the father especially will probably provide warm and proud response as the child shows independence, initiative and self-control, and this response may be hypothesized to bolster the child's sense of *self-determination.* Second, as the child gains greater control over his verbal communication, muscle coordination and aggression, both parents will communicate their approval of these performances, and this should foster a sense of *competence* in the child. Third, the mother will often invest toilet training with moral meaning, so that her rewards and punishments in this area will begin to establish in the child a sense of greater or less moral worth (25a).

Psychoanalytic theory has formulated some of the difficulties of this early childhood period in terms of the 'anal character type' asserted to result from overly harsh and anxious toilet training: orderliness, perseverance, punctuality, cleanliness and stubbornness in milder cases; miserliness, and the idea of the obsessive-compulsive personality in more extreme forms.[2] Parsons and Olds[3] make the further suggestion that 'oversupport' (insufficient limits and urgings toward self-control) may in extreme cases produce the configuration usually diagnosed as manic (compulsive independence). One doesn't need to accept the psychoanalytic assertion of libidinal investment in the anal area in order to see that simultaneous emphasis on compliance with parental expectations and urgings toward self-control of bodily functions and aggression is likely to engender the ambivalences and tempestuous changeableness that mothers ruefully refer to as 'the terrible twos' (23).

Stage III: THE OEDIPAL PERIOD – age 3–5 – EXPRESSIVE AND INSTRUMENTAL THEMES

Traditional sociological approaches to socialization generally begin with this 3–5 age period, because it is during this time that the child's cognitive capacities and cultural learning have developed to the point that language and imagination can be

---

1   T. Lidz, *The Person,* p. 160.
2   E. H. Erikson (ed.), *Identity and the Life Cycle,* p. 72; T. Lidz, *The Person,* pp. 181-3.
3   T. Parsons and J. Olds, 'The mechanisms of personality functioning with special reference to Socialization', p. 256.

used in what has come to be known as the process of *role-taking* (12).[1] George Herbert Mead[2] had originally formulated the very genesis of the self (and of social control) as a two-stage process in which the young child in this 'play stage' first plays the role of various social types in his direct experience (a mother or father, a policeman, a teacher, etc.) and alternately plays the role of himself in reciprocal relation.

Once this idea of constructing reciprocal perspectives is established, the child begins to interpret his own behavior and characteristics from his construction of the perspectives of those actual personages (24). When the child is a little older, he enters a 'game stage' in a peer group context in which he actually plays the various roles in rule-governed games (such as pitcher or catcher in baseball).

In both play and game stages, the child is constructing a view of himself and his characteristics as he *imagines* he would be interpreted from the standpoint of the other in the reciprocal interaction. The essential difference is that the 'other' is a single person in the play stage, but in the game stage is a 'generalized other' making judgments in terms of the impersonal rules (the team as a whole, the other team, the spectators, etc.) (9). Mead's insight that both I (self-as-subject) and Me (self-conceptions, self-as-object) arise only from the symbolic processes of social interaction, as organized into roles, was an important theoretical advance over James M. Baldwin's[3] similar socio-developmental formulation and the more individualistic perspectives on the self of William James.[4] The lifelong importance of an individual's interpretations of significant others' perceptions and attitudes toward him, as partial determinants of his own self-conceptions, had previously been stressed by Charles Horton Cooley (but without the recognition of the completely social birth of the self-processes) in his discussion of the 'looking-glass self', in turn borrowed from a poem by Emerson:

> Each to each a looking-glass
> Reflects the other that doth pass.

As we see our face, figure, and dress in the glass, and are interested in them because they are ours, and pleased or otherwise with them according as they do or do not answer to what we should like them to be; so in imagination we perceive in another's mind some thought of our appearance, manners, aims, deeds, character, friends, and so on, and are variously affected by it. A self-idea of this sort seems to have three principal elements: the imagination of our appearance to the other

---

1 R. H. Turner, 'Role-taking, role standpoint, and reference group behavior', and 'Role-taking: process versus conformity', in A. M. Rose (ed.), *Human Behavior and Social Processes: An Interactionist approach* (Boston, 1962), pp. 20-40; L. S. Cottrell Jr, 'Interpersonal interaction and the development of the self', in D. Goslin (ed.), *Socialization Theory*, pp. 543-70.
2 G. H. Mead, *Mind, Self and Society* (Chicago, 1934), pp. 144-64.
3 J. M. Baldwin, *Social and Ethical Interpretations in Mental Development* (New York, 1897); portions are excerpted in C. Gordon and K. J. Gergen (eds.), *The Self in Social Interaction*, vol. 1, *Classic and Contemporary Perspectives* (New York, 1968).
4 W. James, *Psychology: The Briefer Course* (New York, 1892), ch. 12.

person; the imagination of his judgment of that appearance; and some sort of self-feeling, such as pride or mortification. The comparison with a looking-glass hardly suggests the second element, the imagined judgment, which is quite essential.[1]

The theoretical perspectives provided by James, Baldwin, Cooley and Mead form the basic framework of the symbolic interactionist tradition in sociological social psychology. Their works contain material relevant to role and value development across the life-cycle.[2] The whole idea of an important shift from an early individual world of a play stage with particular others' judgments to interpret, to a much more social world of a game stage, with a generalized other of shared internalized normative standards as an additional perspective of self-judgments, received important corroboration from Piaget's work. Especially in *The Language and Thought of the Child*,[3] but also in other writings,[4] Piaget distinguishes the largely egocentric cognitive patterns of the 'pre-operational sub-period' (about age 2–7) from cognitive patterns of the 'concrete operations sub-period' (about age 7–11) in which children are able to handle problems of combination, separation, conservation of quantity, weight and volume, and other operations involving abstract properties, some logical relations, and a concern with rules. Research on this development continues,[5] and attention is now returning to older problems of the relative effects of race, social class and cognitive environment as determinants of young children's mental development.[6]

Such research focuses on the developing *cognitive capacities* that allow a child to transcend individualized or bi-polar role-taking and to move to forming self-conceptions and self-control utilizing social control through internalization of the generalized other. Unfortunately, such attention would eliminate scrutiny of the entire motivational core of the 3–5 age period unless solid analysis is also focused on the dominating *content* of the period's socialization process: resolution of the oedipal crisis through acquisition of gender-role themes.

As the child's cognitive capacities increase and his muscle coordinations and language learning have reached a level allowing relatively stable interaction, the

1   C. H. Cooley, *Human Nature and the Social Order* (New York, 1902), p. 153.
2   E. Goffman, *The Presentation of Self in Everyday Life* (New York, 1959) and *Asylums* (New York, 1961); A. R. Lindesmith and A. Strauss, *Social Psychology* (New York, 1956); A. L. Strauss, *Mirrors and Masks* (New York, 1959); T. Shibutani, *Society and Personality* (Englewood Cliffs, N.J., 1961), note especially part 4; A. M. Rose (ed.), *Human Behavior*; J. G. Manis and B. N. Meltzer (eds.), *Symbolic Interaction: A Reader in Social Psychology* (Boston, 1967); G. J. McCall and J. L. Simmons, *Identities and Interactions* (New York, 1966); C. Gordon and K. J. Gergen (eds.), *The Self in Social Interaction*, vol. 1.
3   J. Piaget, *The Language and Thought of the Child* (New York, 1926).
4   J. H. Flavell, *Psychology of Jean Piaget*, chs. 4 and 5.
5   Cf. J. S. Bruner *et al.*, *Studies in Cognitive Growth*.
6   M. Deutsch, I. Katz and A. Jensen, *Social Class, Race, and Psychological Development* (New York, 1968); R. D. Hess and R. M. Bear (eds.), *Early Education: Current Theory, Research, and Action* (Chicago, 1968); Harvard Educational Review, 'Environment, heredity, and intelligence' (Spring 1969), a compilation of recent papers.

father is likely to assume a much more active role in the socialization of either a boy or a girl. The father's generally independent and instrumental orientation derived from his own socialization and from his role of 'provider' in relation to the economic world outside the family sets up new value-theme dilemmas for the children, who have been until this time oriented primarily to the dependent and expressive context of relations with their mother. Intense interaction with the father combined with possible sibling rivalry and the newly-developed imaginative role-taking concerning father, mother and their interrelations now set up a different form of gender-role acquisition through identification for boys as compared to girls. Both parents will use their sanctioning powers (rewards and punishments) toward what they see as the proper gender-role for boys and girls. Parsons has delineated the situation with precision:

Then we can say that the boy has to undergo at this stage a *double* 'emancipation'. In common with his sister he has to recognize that, in a sense not previously so important, he must not pretend to adulthood, he is unequivocally a child. But as differentiated from her, he must substitute a new identification with an unfamiliar and in a very important sense threatening object, the father, at the expense of his previous solidarity with his mother . . . Put a little differently, the boy must proceed farther and more radically on the path away from expressive primacy toward instrumental primacy.[1]

Most cultures and sub-cultures make very distinct differentiations between the interaction patterns most highly valued for males and females, and therefore socialization processes will emphasize different value-themes, different priorities, and different subsidiary roles according to the gender of the child (21, 22a). Charges by either parents or peers that the child is a sissy or a tomboy now become important as sanctioning devices, in addition to the general epithet 'baby' for both sexes.

Once again it seems wise to turn to the observations of a socially-oriented psychiatrist with long experience in dealing with children in the 3—5 age range:

The resolution of the oedipal conflict terminates early childhood. The need to rescind the wish to pre-empt a parent brings with it a reorganization of the child's world and a re-evaluation of his place in it. Life will never again be viewed so egocentrically, and fantasy now yields priority to harsh reality. The child has taken a giant step toward becoming an independent and self-sufficient person, even though he has done so by recognizing the long road ahead before he can expect adult prerogatives. He has found peace with both parents by repressing the erotic aspect of his attachment to one. Nevertheless the erotic attachment survives in the unconscious and will become a determinant of later relationships. The precise manner in which the oedipal situation — sometimes called 'the family romance' — has been worked through is likely to set a pattern that will later be relived in different settings.[2]

1 T. Parsons, 'Family structure and socialization of the child', pp. 98-9.
2 T. Lidz, *The Person*, p. 234.

Stage IV: LATER CHILDHOOD – ages 6–11 – COMPETENCE INSTRUCTION FOR PEER RELATIONSHIPS AND EVALUATED ABILITIES

Once the major crises of the oedipal period have been passed, the child begins to participate in a social world much wider than the nuclear family. This process begins with the 'parallel play' with neighborhood children and is often carried on in the various 'readiness' activities of a pre-school. The major change, however, comes with substantial time-commitment to formal schooling, which is oriented around 'work' rather than 'play'. This of course is an intensification of the instrumental themes of the previous period, the essential difference being that now the socialization situation has shifted to one of universalistic, impersonal instruction by teachers and fellow-pupils, from particularistic and intensely personal urgings in the home (15–19).

Cognitive development is much more salient during the 6–11 years, which led Freud to consider them a time of 'latency', or relative calm, between the emotional storms of the oedipal period and adolescence. Interaction with teachers, school and neighborhood peers, parents, television, and printed sources (as 'reading, 'riting, and 'rithmetic' are acquired) indicates the full range of ego functions and the cognitive operations described by Piaget as 'concrete operations'[1] plus a massive diversity of cognitive representations concerning cultural 'facts', assumptions, value-premises, language-usages, technical skills and the like.[2]

Recent works on the acquisition of super-ego functions, in the sense of more extensive moral imperatives of right and wrong than presumably were internalized as parental proscriptions during the oedipal period, are of special sociological significance. The nature and development of the moral orientations (concerning honesty, conscience, fairness, justice, etc.) are in many ways related to the universalism of school and same-age typical peer groups. Very interesting work on childrens' morality has been done by Piaget[3] with special reference to the shift of rules of childrens' games from divine and unchangeable (ages 6–8), to being contractual and quite open to cooperative re-negotiation (ages 11–12). More recently, Kohlberg has been integrating the cognitive structure developmental perspective with consideration of moral norms and controls over conduct, and his formulation of a sequence of stages (amoral, fearful–dependent, opportunistic, conforming-to-persons, conforming-to-rules, and principled–autonomous) may

---

1   J. H. Flavell, *Psychology of Jean Piaget*, ch. 5.
2   A. L. Baldwin, 'A cognitive theory of socialization', in D. Goslin (ed.), *Socialization Theory*, pp. 325-45; B. R. McCandless, 'Childhood socialization'; J. A. Clausen, 'Perspectives on childhood socialization', in J. A. Clausen, *Socialization and Society* (Boston, 1968), pp. 130-81; O. W. Ritchie and M. R. Koller, *Sociology of Childhood* (New York, 1964); J. H. S. Bossard and E. S. Boll, *The Sociology of Child Development* (New York, 1966).
3   J. H. Flavell, *Psychology of Jean Piaget*, pp. 290-7.

provide a guide to solid research across childhood and adolescence.[1] Some investigation of the importance of parental limits in developing self-esteem among children has been conducted by Coopersmith,[2] and the coercive moral power of the same-sex peer groups have been pointed out by many[3] (9, 9a, 9b).

Throughout all the literature on later childhood there runs the theme of tension between the acquisition of competences regarding technical abilities and competences concerning interpersonal relationships (13). In part, this is a matter of the necessary economy of time and attention, in which hours devoted to learning to play the piano or reading about racing-cars, for example, cannot be spent with friends from school or neighborhood. But in a more complex fashion, these skills are learned in social contexts (from girls' 'playing house' to boys' 'working on our bikes'), and the knowledge acquired very often forms the basis for later peer group interaction (13a). Sports of all kinds are obvious cases of this, but so also are uses to which knowledge of 'popular culture' can be put in the intermittent but interminable conversations of children in this 6–11 age bracket.

Erikson[4] frames the central issue of this stage as one of developing a sense of industry versus inferiority. Robert White has elaborated this dimension in terms of mastery and the sense of competence,[5] and Weinstein[6] has applied a very social view of this to interpersonal competence. But in addition to competence, the other three later senses of self are also relevant in the stage of childhood. As was suggested in the previous section, disapproval from peers, teachers or parents is likely to decrease and weaken the child's developing sense of competence, and recent criticisms of urban schools have been directed at just this impact on sensed competence.[7] Acceptance in valued peer groups bolsters the sense of unity. Moral worth concerns are likely to center around issues like cheating or lying, while self-determination will be sensed in stepping beyond the parental limits. Self-esteem is becoming a kind of weighted combination of the four, with competence taking first priority at present (25, 25a, 25b).

---

[1] L. Kohlberg, 'Stage and sequence', pp. 369-89.

[2] S. Coopersmith, *The Antecedents of Self-esteem.*

[3] See the studies reviewed by F. Elkin, *The Child and Society,* pp. 62-70, or O. W. Ritchie and M. R. Koller, *Sociology of Childhood,* especially ch. 12.

[4] E. H. Erikson, 'Growth and crisis of the healthy personality', pp. 82-8.

[5] R. W. White, 'Motivation reconsidered: the concept of confidence', *Psychological Review,* 66 (1959), 297-333 and 'Competence and the psychosexual stages of development', in M. Jones (ed.), *Nebraska Symposium on Motivation* (Lincoln, Nebraska, 1960), pp. 97-141 and 'Ego and reality in psychoanalytical theory', *Psychological Issues* (monograph no. 11, 1963).

[6] E. A. Weinstein, 'The development of interpersonal competence', in D. Goslin (ed.), *Socialization Theory,* pp. 753-75.

[7] Cf. J. Holt, *How Children Fail* (New York, 1964); J. Kozol, *Death at an Early Age* (Boston, 1967); J. I. Roberts (ed.), *School Children in the Urban Slum* (New York, 1967); W. Glasser, *Schools without Failure* (New York, 1969).

Stage V: EARLY ADOLESCENCE – ages 12–15 – ACCEPTANCE/ACHIEVEMENT

A rush of biological maturation brings childhood to a close, and socially-patterned expectations soon provide both problems and solutions, centering mainly around the paradoxically contradictory value-themes of acceptance and achievement. Early adolescence is usually thought to begin with the 'growth-spurt' that produces marked development of the primary and then secondary sex characteristics, a rapid change in the nature of the hormonal secretions, and (of perhaps greater importance) which signals the start of the adolescent's social metamorphosis into a fully sexualized person, capable of producing serious harm as well as significant pleasure.

In girls, this rapid growth produces breast buds at about 9½ or 10 and first menstruation about two years later; in boys, rapid testicular growth starts about 11½, with the development of secondary sex characteristics coming approximately one year later.[1] For both sexes, these first major changes are followed by extremely rapid growth in height and weight, which causes many girls to tower over the boys (who always seem to be about 1½ years behind), and makes both sexes awkward and very concerned with the uncertain arts of impression management.

General cognitive development reaches the full extent of its structural differentiation in what Piaget has designated as the formal operations (achieved in the ages 11–15), and concerns thought about hypothetical possibilities, propositions stating implications, and operations upon operations, as in the analysis of possible combinations of elements.[2] From a sociological point of view, it is interesting to note that this type of formal thought (such as algebra or geometry) was just what Bernstein[3] found very difficult for lower-working-class young people in England, whereas matched groups of middle-class students could handle this formal mode of thought *in addition* to the shared 'public' language. It is also possible that the capacity to handle cognitively these combinations of not yet visible but abstractly possible events may be connected to the more distant aspirations of middle-class adolescents.[4]

One of the main social contexts of the early adolescent period is the shift from the neighborhood elementary school to the more distant junior high school and eventually (in urban areas) to a relatively centralized high school. The family's social class, ethnicity (22a), and more directly interactional effects can be seen in

1   E. Douvan and M. Gold, 'Modal patterns in American adolescence', in L. W. and M. L. Hoffman, *Child Development,* vol. 2, pp. 572-5.
2   J. H. Flavell, *Psychology of Jean Piaget,* ch. 6.
3   B. Bernstein, 'Social class and linguistic development; a theory of social learning', in A. H. Halsey, J. Floud and C. A. Anderson (eds.), *Education, Economy and Society* (New York, 1961).
4   C. Gordon, 'Looking ahead; self-conceptions, race and family factors as determinants of adolescent achievement orientations', American Sociological Association Monograph Series, in press; and 'Social characteristics of early adolescence', *Daedalus* (Fall 1971), in press.

relation to the early adolescent's level of self-esteem.[1] Parents and siblings are still of very great importance, and the grandparent generation may have strong impact in guiding the early adolescent, but now some of the main roles are changing and a new component of responsibility is being added (14a).[2] The 'child' component of the 'son' and 'daughter' roles is disappearing, and the young adolescent boy may become furious if his sister introduces him as her 'little brother'.

Own-sex peer groups drawn from the school now become very engrossing, so that the role of 'member' becomes elaborated (15). The same-sex 'best friend' pattern provides emotional security as a basis for more extensive relations involving the issue of acceptance. Since parents and peers alike invest all sorts of sexual activity with moral meaning, it can be hypothesized that the sense of moral worth will be related to the interpretation of his sexual status made by the adolescent's significant others. High schools and junior high schools are also significant social contexts in that their 'official' culture embodies the value-theme of achievement (that is, *performance* measured against standards of excellence) in addition to the continuing stress upon valued *qualities* such as ethnicity, social class, and gender-role attributes such as sexual attractiveness.[3] Thus the role of 'student' takes on special meaning as an achievement (since some peers are already failing or dropping out of school), and as a performance dimension (in the sense of 'good' student and 'poor' student) (13).

The interrelations between acceptance and achievement can be seen throughout the literature on early adolescence, from Hollingshead's *Elmtown's Youth* through Coleman's *The Adolescent Society* and on into the broad range of recent material.[4]

Acceptance, or *symbolically validated membership and welcomed participation* in a group's important interaction patterns can refer to the family, to the peer crowd or clique, to 'official' school groups, or to the wider world of social class, socioeconomic status and ethnic subcultures. Likewise, achievement, or *symbolically validated performance against a standard of comparison, competition or excellence* can take place in any of these social arenas.

---

1   M. Rosenberg, *Society and the Adolescent Self-Image* (Princeton, N.J., 1963); C. Gordon, *Looking Ahead.*
2   Y. Cohen, *The Transition from Childhood to Adolescence* (Chicago, 1964).
3   T. Parsons, 'The school class as a social system: some of its functions in American society', *Harvard Educational Review,* 29 (Fall), 297-318; R. H. Turner, 'Role: sociological aspects'.
4   J. Coleman, *The Adolescent Society* (New York, 1961), pp. 43-50. Cf. P. Goodman, *Growing up Absurd* (New York, 1956); E. Z. Friedenberg, *The Vanishing Adolescent* (New York, 1959) and *Coming of Age in America* (New York, 1967); E. A. Smith, *American Youth Culture* (New York, 1962); J. M. Seidman (ed.), *The Adolescent* (New York, 1960); R. E. Grinder (ed.), *Studies in Adolescence* (New York, 1965); H. Sebald, *Adolescence: a sociological analysis* (New York, 1968); G. Caplan and S. Lebovici (eds.), *Adolescence: Psychological Perspectives* (New York, 1969); E. G. Campbell, 'Adolescent socialization', in D. Goslin (ed.), *Handbook of Socialization.* More general work on achievement can be found in D. C. McClelland *et al., The Achievement Motive* (New York, 1953), B. C. Rosen, H. J. Crockett and C. Z. Nunn, *Achievement in American Society* (Cambridge, Mass., 1969); R. L. Coser (ed.), *Life Cycle and Achievement in America* (New York, 1969).

D

There is inherent contradiction between acceptance and achievement in that some of the most visible forms of achievement, such as making high grades in school, rank quite low as grounds for popularity, and in that peer group and dating activities that engender and maintain popularity take large amounts of time away from studying. Coleman's study of some 7,000 Illinois high school students in 1957 does show, however, that certain forms of achievement do form important grounds for *increased* popularity, especially for boys. Having high grades was ranked quite low by the students as a basis for popularity for boys and even lower for girls. Being an athlete, being in the 'leading crowd' and being a leader in activities were the most important criteria for boys, and being in the leading crowd, being a leader in activities and having nice clothes were most important for girls.[1]

While these priorities have altered somewhat in recent years, it is quite probable that newer evidence would still document the continuation of cultural emphasis on value-theme dispositions established in the oedipal period. During the time of early adolescence, the boys show an increasing devotion of energy to the achievement and independence area, receiving in return *approval* to support the sense of competence, and *response* to support the sense of self-determination (Gordon, 1970). The girls are increasingly directed toward the development of interpersonal skills, which yield approval and also the acceptance that increases the sense of unity.[2]

Thus recognition for performances and qualities that are valued in both official and peer cultures can resolve the paradox and dilemma of acceptance and achievement. Many social types in the informal pantheon of American high school culture articulate this double-valued recognition, such as the 'Big Wheel' and the 'Gentleman Jock' (21). Perhaps there is also a kind of reverse or residual resolution of the acceptance/achievement problem: if (as high school football coaches are likely to convey) it is true that 'nice guys finish last', then do last guys finish nice?

To a significant extent, the period of early adolescence represents a series of attempts by these 12—16 year olds to gain some autonomy from their parents while gaining peer support through conformity to the 'teenage' or 'youth-culture' norms.[3] However, the totality of commitment to acceptance in this peer society has been greatly overstated, to the near-exclusion of the personal ambitions that make themselves very strongly evident in later adolescence (26). Turner has provided a better perspective:

In sum, the youth subculture is a segmental and ritual pattern which many youth enact in the spirit of a game while still retaining private standards and goals at variance with it. On the one hand, the pattern provides a ready identity for the individual in an otherwise amorphous situation and protects the individual by

1   C. Gordon, 'Social characteristics of early adolescence'.
2   E. Douvan and M. Gold, 'Modal patterns in American adolescence', pp. 194-5; E. Douvan and J. Avelson, *The Adolescent Experience* (New York, 1966), chs. 2, 7 and 10.
3   See for example E. A. Smith, *American Youth Culture* (New York, 1962); and E. Douvan and J. Avelson, *The Adolescent Experience*.

imposing controls on his peer environment. On the other hand, the special youth interests provide a basis for sociable enjoyment and a considerable degree of fellow-feeling. The ritual forms of interaction and subjects of communication provide a means for ready communication in casual and fleeting interpersonal relations. The declarations against success in fields of serious accomplishment are hardly to be taken other than as public disavowals to protect the individual's pride in the face of possible failure in highly valued pursuits.[1]

Stage VI: LATER ADOLESCENCE – ages 16–20 – IDENTITY FORMATION TO BRIDGE THE INTIMACY/AUTONOMY DILEMMA

The differentiation of roles and social types that began in early adolescence becomes much more complex and fateful in the ages of 16–20. High school, college and work-setting sub-cultures are abundantly supplied with these key symbolic mechanisms of socialization and social control (1, 2, 21). Klapp has formulated the nature and functioning of this layer of cultural meanings with great clarity in his discussion of the ways in which *praise* (communicated by hero typing), *condemnation* (through typing as a villain), and *ridicule* (for those typed as fools) contribute to role discrimination, definition and institutionalization of emergent roles, professionalization, provision of self-images, control by status modification, and elevation of general consensus[2] (16–18). Some version of such types as Big Wheel, Jock, Great Lover, Brain, Socialite, Hood, Grind, and Freak probably exists at every high school and college campus, and every substantial work-setting has its cautionary tales about Ratebusters, Brown-nosers and Goof-offs (3, 10).

These informal sub-cultural typifications of salient modes of relation to authority, prestige, work, sex and achievement should not be taken lightly, because they tell a good deal about the open and covert concerns of the members of the little sub-societies into which the late adolescent is being socialized. Also, if only by avoidance, these social-type constructs help to establish the dimensions and even some of the contents of the self-and-other conceptions or identity fragments that the late adolescent is acquiring.

Many more formal and more widely understood and sanctioned roles have become relevant by age 16. Increasingly, these roles involve important components of *autonomy* in the sense of independent decision or choice about whether to engage in the relevant action, and *responsibility* in the sense of being held accountable for the outcomes of that action. This new imputation of responsible autonomy is well symbolized by the granting of a driver's license (in most states at age 16). The most important of the new roles relate to more differentiated versions of the achievement and acceptance themes of the prior period, dealing prominently

[1] R. H. Turner, *The Social Context of Ambition* (San Francisco, 1964), p. 146.
[2] O. A. Klapp, *Heroes, Villians and Fools* (Englewood Cliffs, N.J., 1962), pp. 16–18.

with work, sexuality, joyful experiences, honesty, legality, philosophy, politics, and the like – all now serious concerns with fateful consequences. Consider some of the possibilities, and their likely implications if the young person enacting them should run afoul of the society's legal machinery, charged with detecting and punishing whatever is currently being defined as deviance: marijuana user or seller, swinger, drop-out, 'teenage driver', pacifist, hood, violent protester, militant radical, etc., etc.

Such roles and their 'straight' complements or counterparts play an important part in the self-conceptions of late adolescents,[1] and represent a major theme of seeking or avoiding personal autonomy and its entailed responsibility. Lidz once again is worth quoting on some of the psychodynamics underlying the autonomy struggle of the late adolescent:

He must prove to himself that he is capable and does not need to rely upon his parents' judgment and advice. Nevertheless, his own inner directives derive largely from internalizations of his parents and their standards and directives. Such inner restrictions must be overcome as much as, or more than, the actual limitations set by the parents. The superego must be reconstituted in order to become suited for directing adult rather than childhood behavior; loosened to permit greater latitude but at the same time strengthened to become capable of directing the self with less supervision from parents (24).[2]

Just as peer group acceptance provided emotional and social support for developing increased freedom *from* parental controls in early adolescence, so the freedom *to* make one's own way is encouraged by the increasing degree of *intimacy* in both friendship and love. This provides a 'psycho-social moratorium'[3] in which ideas, roles and relationships can be tested without the threat of failure or long-term commitment. Whether in the form of the emotional and sexual intimacy of the love-relationship or in the more pragmatic mutuality of streetcorner men,[4] the importance of intimacy would be hard to over-estimate. In the late adolescent period many of the components of the search for intimacy may be seen in the young person's embracing one or more ideological causes or sub-aspects of 'The Movement'. A poignant glimpse of the intricate relations between the autonomy and intimacy value-complexes may be found by comparing two recent books by Kenneth Keniston: *The Uncommitted: Alienated Youth in American Society* and *Young Radicals: Notes on Committed Youth.*[5]

So much has been written on the effects of college on students that a recent summary and synthesis fills two volumes and covers a 75-page bibliography.[6]

1 C. Gordon, 'Systemic senses of self'.
2 T. Lidz, *The Person*, p. 327.
3 E. H. Erikson, 'The problem of ego identity', p. 164.
4 E. Liebow, *Tally's Corner* (Boston, 1966).
5 K. Keniston, *The Uncommitted: Alienated Youth in American Society* (New York, 1960) and *Young Radicals: Notes on Committed Youth* (New York, 1968).
6 K. A. Feldman and T. M. Newcomb, *The Impact of College on Students* (2 vols., San Francisco, 1969).

Although the mass of detail is bewildering, there does emerge a major pattern of change associated with the college experience (apart from the substantial increases in cognitive information, and a very general process of maintenance and accentuation of the particular value-patterns and inter-personal style that the students had acquired before they entered college):

Declining 'authoritarianism', dogmatism, and prejudice, together with decreasingly conservative attitudes toward public issues and growing sensitivity to aesthetic experiences, are particularly prominent forms of change – as inferred from freshman–senior differences. These add up to something like increasing openness to multiple aspects of the contemporary world, paralleling wider ranges of contact and experience. Somewhat less consistently, but nevertheless evident, are increasing intellectual interests and capacities, and declining commitment to religion, especially in its more orthodox forms. Certain kinds of personal changes – particularly toward *greater independence, self-confidence,* and *readiness to express impulses* – are the rule rather than the exception.[1]

The struggle for autonomy concerns just this confident independence, and the readiness to express impulses is at the heart of the search for intimacy.

Whether the focus is on the contentions, conflicts and compromises of student politics,[2] on the more private domain of occupational aspirations, choices and preparations,[3] or on the attempts by increasing numbers of young people to transform the adult world before it crushes or destroys them,[4] the value-themes of autonomy and intimacy are of crucial significance.

Erikson has crystallized the way in which identity formation brings together the person's developing constellation of all kinds of identity fragments ('constitutional givens, idiosyncratic libidinal needs, favored capacities, significant identifications, effective defenses, successful sublimations, and consistent roles') to bridge the intimacy/autonomy dilemma of late adolescence:

The integration now taking place in the form of the ego identity is more than the sum of the childhood identifications. It is the inner capital accrued from all those experiences of each successive stage, when successful identification led to a successful alignment of the individual's *basic drives* with his *endowment* and his *opportunities*. In psychoanalysis we ascribe such successful alignments to 'egosynthesis'; I have tried to demonstrate that the ego values accrued in childhood culminate in what I have called *a sense of ego identity*. The sense of ego identity,

---

1   *Ibid.* Italics added.
2   S. M. Lipset (ed.), *Student Politics* (New York, 1967).
3   J. A. Davis, *Great Aspirations* (Chicago, 1964) and *Undergraduate Career Decisions* (Chicago, 1965).
4   Cf. E. H. Erikson (ed.), *The Challenge of Youth* (New York, 1961); K. Keniston, *Young Radicals*; J. Newfield, *The Prophetic Minority* (New York, 1967); B. M. Berger, 'The new stage of American man – almost endless adolescence', *New York Times Magazine* (2nd Nov. 1969), pp. 32ff.; T. Roszak, *The Making of a Counter Culture: Reflections on the Technocratic Society and its Youthful Opposition* (Garden City, New York, 1969); C. A. Reich, *The Greening of America*.

then, is the accrued confidence that one's ability to maintain inner sameness and continuity (one's ego in the psychological sense) is matched by the sameness and continuity of one's meaning for others. Thus, self-esteem, confirmed at the end of each major crisis, grows to be a conviction that one is learning effective steps toward a tangible future, that one is developing a defined personality within a social reality which one understands (25b, 25a).[1]

Stage VII: YOUNG ADULTHOOD – ages 21–29 – CONNECTION/SELF-DETERMINATION

Although age 18 marks the point at which young men are currently thought old enough to die in the defense of the country or in pursuit of its foreign policy objectives, it is age 21 that marks the formal assumption of the rights of *legal* adulthood (including the right to partake of the society's approved psycho-active chemicals) and full voting citizenship. The 21st birthday can serve as an arbitrary starting point in this stage of the life-cycle, yet there are two much more significant role acquisitions that actually bring about the transition from adolescence to young adulthood. Freud put it perfectly when asked what he thought a normal person should be able to do well: 'Lieben und arbeiten' he said ('to love and to work').[2]

Entrance into some instrumental occupation (or into preparation for a future occupation in the case of the increasing number of graduate students) usually comes after completion of college at about age 21, and will probably come a good deal earlier for those who did not complete college, served a term in the military, or dropped out of high school. Entrance into legal marriage or some other form of relatively stable expressive bond and living-arrangement also most frequently occurs within a few years of reaching legal adulthood and full citizenship. Occupation and marriage roles are not of necessity the only opportunities for working and loving, but they do form two of the person's most solid bonds to the society's institutional structure (5). For the young man, occupation will determine social class, the content of daily activity, the nature of his associates and companions, the scope of his decisions or power, and the level of his monetary income (17). For the young wife, as for her husband, the marriage (or other such arrangement) will go a long way toward establishing the level of emotional as well as economic security. The nature and integrity of the bonds between the man and the woman will be vital in determining the moral standing of both in the eyes of their parental families, friends and neighbors (19).

Brim[3] has made a strong case that adult socialization is primarily concerned with imparting the content and technique of overt role behavior rather than with inculcating values or motivations, which were the main emphases of childhood socialization. In addition, Brim points out that adult socialization tends to center

---

1   E. H. Erikson, 'Growth and crisis of the healthy personality', p. 89.
2   *Ibid.* p. 96.
3   O. G. Brim Jr, 'Socialization through the life cycle', in O. G. Brim Jr and S. Wheeler, *Socialization after Childhood: Two essays* (New York, 1966).

on acquiring and polishing new combinations of previously learned responses, on practical realism rather than idealism in role prescriptions, on mediation between conflicting role demands, and on specification of learning down to patterns that apply to only a very few situations (20).

These features quite aptly characterize most of the research on occupational socialization (see for example the wide range of materials on socialization for careers in large organizations collected by Glaser,[1] and the thorough review by Moore.[2] Yet it is also true that there remain for young adults important areas of *anticipatory* socialization,[3] in which the major values and some of the behavior patterns of members of significant reference groups are learned as a prelude to possible membership in these groups (see also Biddle and Thomas[4] and Hyman and Singer,[5] for other instances of reference group implications for socialization). The principle of role-taking as an outcome of interaction with significant others would make for this kind of value acquisition as young men begin to deal directly with their next higher-level supervisors (18, 12).

Socialization for the marital relationship is less institutionalized in contemporary, urban America than is the socialization for any other major role.[6] Young people typically have only the emotion-laden models of their own parents, a little advice from married friends, romantic moonbeams from the mass media, and a bewildering array of 'how to' books on everything from sex to cooking. Socialization for parenthood is a good deal more thorough and multi-faceted in that both partners themselves have been children, have probably helped in caring for younger brothers or sisters, will get a much greater quantity of more practical advice from relatives and friends (since this will seem less intrusive and prying than will advice on husband–wife relationships), and will have access to much better advice in the very widely-read 'baby books' (at present these include most prominently Spock, and Ginnott[7]). In addition to social structural factors that cause socialization for marriage and parenthood to be less formally established and substantially reinforced,[8] it may well be that the central value-theme dilemma of young adulthood is at once exceptionally privatized and yet almost irrevocably fateful for his social destiny.

1 B. G. Glaser (ed.), *Organizational Careers: A Sourcebook for Theory* (Chicago, 1968).
2 W. Moore, 'Occupational socialization', in D. Goslin (ed.), *Socialization Theory*.
3 R. K. Merton, *Social Theory and Social Structure* (New York, 1957), pp. 265ff.
4 B. J. Biddle and E. J. Thomas (eds.), *Role Theory: Concepts and Research* (New York, 1966).
5 H. H. Hyman and E. Singer (eds.), *Readings in Reference Group Theory and Research* (New York, 1968).
6 See L. Rainwater, 'Crucible of identity: The Negro lower-class family', *Daedalus,* 95 (1966), 172-216; E. Liebow, *Tally's Corner.*
7 B. Spock, *Doctor Spock Talks with Mothers: Growth and Guidance* (Boston, 1961); H. G. Ginnott, *Between Parent and Child: New Solutions for Old Problems* (New York, 1965).
8 R. Hill and J. Aldous, 'Socialization for marriage and parenthood', in D. Goslin (ed.), *Socialization Theory*; H. H. Perlman, *Persona: Social Role and Personality* (Chicago, 1968), chs. 4 and 5; T. Lidz, *The Person.*

This dilemma concerns the interplay of self-determination and connection. Even when factors of ethnicity, social class, educational preparation, geographical location and personality orientations are taken into account, there still remains a very large range of possible occupations and marriage-partners available to almost any young adult. Just how to maintain the maximum level of self-directed choice regarding future objectives, while in the present establishing these necessary and/or rewarding, stable, and binding connections to the larger social order is an intensely private and frequently painful problem. The problem is magnified because the more self-determining occupations such as the professions generally make demands that put severe strains on the marriage bonds, and the obligations of marriage and parenthood may overwhelm even the most self-determining young men and women (22, 23). Probably most persons never do reach any resolution of this dilemma, as is suggested by the prevalence and demand for specialized agencies of *re*-socialization in just these key areas of occupation (adult education, employment-counseling, and direct job-training), marriage (social work and marriage-counseling), and parenthood (nursery-school, 'Head Start' programs, and child-psychology clinics where there is only a slight attempt to mask the fact that the parents are the patients).

A focused commitment (for the woman as well as for the man) to work, that is personally fulfilling as well as adequately supportive of the family unit, coupled with increased assistance for the marital partners in spreading the burdens and the joys of child-rearing is probably the ideal solution, but is unlikely to be found very frequently under present circumstances (6—9). Lidz has put the problem with unusual clarity:

The young adult's energies and interests can now be directed beyond his own growth and development. His independence from his natal family requires that he achieve an interdependence with others and find his place in the social system. Through vocation and marriage he is united to networks of persons, finds tasks that demand involvement, and gains roles into which he fits and is fitted which help define his identity. He is virtually forced to become less self-centred through the very pursuit of his own interests.[1]

Stage VIII: EARLY MATURITY — ages 30—44 — STABILITY/ ACCOMPLISHMENT

In the ideal—typical case under consideration, once the middle-class (or often working-class) husband gets reasonably well settled in an occupation or started out on a professional career, and once his wife has withdrawn from the work she was doing (while he was finishing his education and before she had their first child), and once they are reasonably well settled in raising their children, there is likely to come a prolonged period when the husband devotes his maximum energies to achievement and advancement in his work (15). This can be a time of very strong productivity

[1]   *Ibid.* p. 363.

or of ultimately futile motion, but in any case the amount of time, attention and motivation devoted by the husband to his efforts will probably cause severe strain within the marital family (22a). Working nights and weekends, taking extended trips, and talking endlessly with partners, colleagues or staff members are likely to increase the wife's feeling of resentment, frustration, and perhaps also her suspicions.

On the contrary, many middle-class men during this period will feel the pull of family concerns and the important necessities of child-rearing tugging at their time schedules to such an extent that they indicate in various subtle ways to their employers and to their competitors that they are not willing or able to apply every last measure of energy to accomplishment-efforts (23). Aspirations will slowly be brought into line with sensed limitations and changing orientations. In another conflictful adaptation, the wife may urge her husband toward greater achievement than he feels he is capable of attaining.

In some circumstances, the twin value-themes of stability and accomplishment can be mutually supporting, as in the case where a substantial promotion provides money enough for purchase of a more desired home and then the wife's happiness and security concerning her children's increased opportunities makes her more supportive of the husband's further efforts. In any case, the approval he receives for his accomplishments will tend to raise his sense of competence, while the acceptance shown by his wife will tend to support his sense of unity (25a). In a great many middle-class occupations, the period around age 45 represents establishment of the high-water mark of motivation and achievement, but in others it may only be a brief plateau.[1] Whether or not the limits of youth's expansiveness have been reached, these years are a constant tension between accomplishment and stability, with occasional opportunities for consolidation of gains.

Stage IX: FULL MATURITY — approximately age 45—65 or retirement — DIGNITY/CONTROL

Somewhere around age 45, many men begin to complain of physical problems that prompt them to 'slow down' in their work and more vigorous recreational activities. These problems may concern difficulties in catching their breath after exertion, backaches or headaches associated with tension or boredom, or one of the many complications of the heart or arteries that plague persons of this age. Among women, the menopause also tends to occur at this age or just a little later, just about the time that the last child has become independent and left home. Whether these physical or health changes are actual 'causes' or simply given special attention

[1]   C. Bühler and F. Massarik (eds.), *The Course of Human Life,* ch. 3; H. S. Becker and A. L. Strauss, 'Careers, personality, and adult socialization', *American Journal of Sociology,* 62 (Nov. 1956), 253-63; L. D. Gain Jr, 'Life course and social structure', in R. E. L. Faris (ed.), *Handbook of Modern Sociology* (Chicago, 1964), pp. 272-309.

as plausible 'reasons', there is a very common tendency for both men and women to focus on them and to sense that the major climb toward accomplishments and connections has been completed or secured, leaving something of a 'coasting' or even 'down-hill' orientation toward the future (26). Lidz has captured the feeling beautifully:

The passage over the crest of life is a particularly critical period, a time of summing up in preparation for the second half of adulthood, and as such, a time of further integration or reintegration. In the transition from adolescence to early adulthood, the individual had become committed to a way of life, he has now lived it and is now mature — or is unlikely ever to become mature. Now, approaching the divide, he looks back and also tries to prognosticate on the basis of his experience. Perhaps he will try to climb still higher, change course while he still can, or decide upon which path of descent is safest. Whether a person makes the most of the opportunity available or whether he begins to die slowly depends upon a wide variety of personality factors, but they continue to include attitudes related to the confidence, trust, and initiative inculcated in the earliest years. The realization that the turn toward the end of life has been rounded awakens anxiety and despair in proportion to feelings that one has never really lived and loved.[1]

Bernice Neugarten is one of the few social scientists who has been concerned with pursuing research and theory on the later stages of the life-cycle, and has performed a valuable service by bringing together her original work with that of others in a single volume, under the title *Middle Age and Aging*.[2] One research report after another (see esp. Parts I–III) documents the generalization that *control* of one's own skills and decisions, resources, organizations, and of other persons, is a central and crucial value-theme among the fully mature. This is most accentuated among middle-class respondents and among men, but it is quite apparent in other groups as well. The strands of competence and self-determination (fostered respectively by continued approval and acquiescence) that we have been following since childhood are now seen in highly differentiated and yet integrated form. One of Neugarten's respondents in a study of upper middle-class middle-aged persons said:

There is a difference between wanting to *feel* young and wanting to *be* young. Of course it would be pleasant to maintain the vigor and appearance of youth; but I would not trade those things for the authority or the autonomy I feel — no, nor the ease of interpersonal relationships nor the self-confidence that comes from experience.[3]

1   T. Lidz, *The Person*, p. 473.
2   B. L. Neugarten, *Middle Age and Aging* (Chicago, 1968). See for instance her 'Adult personality: toward a psychology of the life cycle' in the above, pp. 137-47.
3   B. L. Neugarten, 'The awareness of middle age', in R. Owen (ed.), *Middle Age* (London, 1967).

The theme of autonomous control over some defined sphere of social life (whether in an occupational sense or in relation to dependent children) is largely directed toward taking active responsibility for future events within that sphere. But there is also another major theme running through the literature on the full maturity period: *dignity,* the desire for respect accorded on the basis of *past* accomplishments, sacrifices and services. This can be inferred in part from the tendency for persons in the full maturity period to think of their age (and of time in general) in terms of the time *remaining* until death rather than in terms of the time that has *passed* since their birth.[1] When life is seen as drawing to a close, and as coping capacities are seen as declining, the tendency to 'rest on one's laurels' becomes stronger and anxiety may become more intense. This period of life also contains several role-shifts that move the individual toward integrative and pattern-maintenance activities and away from major achievements and decision-making at all but the highest levels of large organizations (15). The roles of grandmother and grandfather, advisory board-member, staff consultant, sponsor (for the mobility efforts of younger colleagues), and the executive who has been 'kicked upstairs' to a figurehead position are all instances of roles that provide dignity; in these cases *respect* for valued *past* accomplishments (supporting the sense of moral worth) tends to replace *approval* for highly competent current and expected achievement (supporting the sense of competence) as the predominant symbolic medium in interaction.

As long as the person has *some* valued and structurally significant role to enact, he can probably maintain a more or less precarious balance between instrumental control and expressive dignity, especially where he feels integrity in his position and receives recognition for his importance (both past and future) to the significant others around him. Yet this kind of recognition is not readily available to the vast majority of men and women whose occupational roles have never been particularly self-involving, let alone sources of lofty symbolic rewards. Until changes in occupational opportunity structures and adult socialization occur, middle-, working- and lower-class people will have to draw upon family and other institutional spheres, as even the least rewarding work-life role is ultimately given up (13a). This situation has serious consequences, both individual and social; in Erikson's terms:

Despair expresses the feeling that the time is short, too short for the attempt to start another life and to try out alternative roads to integrity. Such a despair is often hidden behind a show of disgust, a misanthropy, or a chronic contemptuous displeasure with particular institutions and particular people – a disgust and a displeasure which (where not allied with constructive ideas and a life of cooperation) only signify the individual's contempt of himself.[2]

---

1   B. L. Neugarten, 'Adult personality', pp. 140-1.
2   E. H. Erikson, 'Growth and crises of the healthy personality', p. 98.

Stage X: OLD-AGE — retirement-age to death — MEANINGFUL INTEGRATION/AUTONOMY

Up until the end of the full maturity stage, the course of the typical life-cycle has clearly been one of increasing *development* — in the value-free sense of increasing differentiation of meanings and acquisition of psychic structure, plus social roles, coupled with integration of the differentiated sub-structures at both psychic and social levels. From the initial moment of conception, the human organism has progressed through a series of reasonably distinct and unevenly paced stages. Cognitive capacities (interacting with cognitive cultural information) also were shown to follow this same pattern of time-phased differentiation and subsequent integration into a configuration of moderately stable equilibrium, followed by successive crisis points of further differentiation. The third strand in the drama of development concerned the affective or motivational differentiation and integration, with special reference to personality trend, and the value-complexes that are the central concern of motivational socialization at each stage. Fourth and finally, the basic sociological framework for all other developments was shown to be the socio-culturally provided structure of reciprocal roles, first linking the socializee to the socializing agents, and then adding important new differentiating and integrating elements as the person being socialized acquired more and more of the available roles (1, 24).

In contrast to earlier development, the predominant feature of the old-age period (roughly beginning with retirement-age and extending until the time of death) is an inexorable *de-differentiation* along each of the four dimensions of the person as an action system: social roles, cognitive or cultural orientation, personality trends and affective dispositions, and bodily health.

The order of the de-differentiations is completely variable in principle, but (barring severe accidents) the predominant pattern seems to be the following: First, social roles are lost, taken away, or voluntarily relinquished. This happens in a rough sequence involving some order of retirement, widowhood, loss of friends or relatives through death, withdrawal from various memberships as activities become too much of a burden, and perhaps giving up being a resident of a specific neighborhood by moving to a retirement area residence or into some kind of special-care facility, and perhaps relinquishment of a wide range of roles that structure the use of time.

Some new roles may be acquired after retirement (such as voluntary association member, author, or great-grandfather, etc.), but the main trend is clearly toward role loss, especially after age 75.[1] This structural and interactional change has been

---

[1] R. J. Havighurst, B. L. Neugarten and S. S. Tobin, 'Disengagement and patterns of aging', in B. L. Neugarten (ed.), *Middle Age and Aging,* pp. 161-72; M. W. Riley and A. Foner *et al., Aging and Society,* vol. 1, *An Inventory of Research Findings* (New York, 1968); pp. 413-14; K. W. Back and K. J. Gergen, 'The self through the latter span of life', in C. Gordon and K. J. Gergen (eds.), *The Self in Social Interaction.*

interpreted by some theorists[1] in terms of a 'disengagement', or willing and even pleasurably relieved laying-down of unwanted burdens of role-governed interaction, coming as the result of a turning-inward of affect and cognition. While there are no doubt many instances in which this is the governing process (especially in very advanced years), the preponderance of research evidence indicates that general life satisfaction, morale and self-esteem are *higher* among those actively linked to others by important social roles, even after age and health have been controlled.[2]

A further crucial factor is that retirement income may be only 25–50 per cent of the pre-retirement level. The actual causal sequence may more frequently be that role loss through retirement, widowhood, death of loved ones, residential moving or physical disability cuts the person loose from the socially structured expectations and activities that provided much of the meaning for his life, thus forcing him to turn his interests and emotions inward.

In addition to the personal tragedies, there are important questions of public policy involved in these questions because of the present low levels of retirement income and social security payments, limits on additional income, inadequate medical care and lagging programs of housing for the elderly, etc. Although it is clear that life-long socialization has taught that purposeful activity and role relationships are the essential content and structure of life, recent social science research is showing that there is *no* viable role of 'old person' *per se,* nor really many important sub-roles to enact. In the vast majority of cases, older people are forced to turn toward their immediate families and eventually inward toward themselves for sustaining roles, resources and relationships.[3] Thus a negative corollary should be added to Turner's exposition of propositions 1, 2, 24 and 25: as roles are relinquished, behavior, sentiment, motives, meaningfulness of events and self-conceptions tend to become disorganized.

Cognitive and affective patterns, the second and third dimensions of de-differentiation in old age, are interrelated in a complex fashion with each other and with role changes. With the advanced years come substantial declines in the sensorimotor areas of vision, hearing, reaction time and general mental ability, including memory and learning capacities.[4] Although research is less solid concerning changes in affective orientations and self-conceptions, there is general consensus among social gerontologists that (compared to younger adults) those of 65 and older tend to be more rigid, dogmatic, intolerant of ambiguity, restrained, cautious, passive, introverted, concerned with their bodily functioning and lower

---

1   Especially E. Cumming and W. E. Henry, *Growing Old* (New York, 1961).
2   M. W. Riley and A. Foner *et al., Aging and Society,* pp. 415-19.
3   P. Townsend, *The Family Life of Old People* (New York, 1957); R. H. Williams and C. G. Wirths, *Lives Through the Years* (New York, 1965); E. Shanas and G. F. Streib (eds.), *Social Structure and the Family: Generational Relations* (Englewood Cliffs, N.J., 1965); I. Rosow, *Social Integration of the Aged* (New York, 1967); B. L. Neugarten, *Middle Age and Aging,* part 5; M. W. Riley and A. Foner *et al., Aging and Society,* part 4; C. Gordon and K. J. Gergen (eds.), *The Self in Social Interaction.*
4   M. W. Riley and A. Foner *et al., Aging and Society,* ch. 11.

in affect, although it should be noted that these are comparisons among different groups of people, not changes in given individuals.[1] No conclusive research has untangled the relation of these patterns as being causes or effects of relinquishing social roles, but it is very suggestive that people who have undergone sharp discontinuity in role relationships (such as becoming a widow or retiring) are much more likely to identify themselves as 'old' or 'elderly', with all the negative imagery these stereotypes hold in American culture.[2] Retirement seems to be the most crucial of these major role changes for men, because our instrumentally-oriented culture places such great value on a man's occupation as a measure of his competence, self-determination and moral worth (25b, 25a). The culture holds 'You are what you do'; by implication, if you *do* nothing, you *are* nothing.

Finally, the advancing years after age 65 are very likely to bring a series of health problems, both minor and severe.[3] Almost 40 per cent of Americans now pick up some kind of physical impairment between age 65 and 75, and after age 75 some 60 per cent will have at least one serious impairment, very often caused by a fall or other accident. The incidence of arthritis, rheumatism, heart difficulties and high blood-pressure increase dramatically with age. Medical progress has been able to reduce the toll from infectious diseases and some other causes so that persons age 65 and over in 1970 will make up about 9.5 per cent of the U.S. population, as compared to about 4.1 per cent in 1900. This total of approximately 19.5 million persons aged 65 or over (up more than six times from the 3 million of 1900) is almost as large as the number of blacks in the nation. Since the projections for 1980 estimate a total of 23,000,000 people over 65 (10 per cent of the U.S. population), the coming years may see the development of a 'grey power' movement directed toward securing social and economic justice for this other disadvantaged minority. While the average number of years of life remaining after age 65 is now about 13 for white men and 16 for white women, death eventually comes to all. Only about 4 per cent of older people are institutionalized for long periods; heart disease and cancer together account for about two out of three of the deaths and these diseases tend to run their courses rather quickly.

Our socialization processes do not really prepare even fully mature adults for the shock and trauma of retirement, widowhood, isolation, loneliness, invalidism or death. Partly this stems from the fact that our culture provides no viable role of 'old person' to be socialized *into,* only the vital and resource-laden roles to be thrust *out of,* with little concern for re-structuring meanings by socialization even then. Of very great benefit would be the development of new roles for the elderly that would draw upon their vast reserves of now wasted motivation and competence to provide forms of humane service to those in need of advice, experience and understanding.

1   *Ibid.* ch. 12.
2   *Ibid.* pp. 302-11.
3   *Ibid.* chs. 2 and 9.

Two final value-complexes stand out in the literature on the old-age period and in my interviews with elderly persons — two themes that run counter to the loss of roles and resources, inward turning of interests, and physical decline. These are the partially contradictory but also possibly mutually supportive themes of *autonomy* and *meaningful integration.*

The *sense of personal autonomy* concerns self-sufficiency in the setting and attainment of one's own goals, whatever might be their content and level. As such, it fits in the overall structure of self-conceptions at a point more general and abstract than the four systemic senses of self (competence, self-determination, unity and moral worth), but less global than self-esteem.[1]

In terms of the stage-developmental model used here, personal autonomy at the last stage is the logical culmination of the earlier components *self-determination* in young adulthood, *accomplishment* in early maturity, and *control* in full maturity. This follows the same pattern whereby autonomy in later adolescence was seen as developing out of *self-control* in early childhood, *evaluated abilities* in later childhood, and *achievement* in early adolescence. Whether early or late, this sense of personal autonomy relates to the person's intermittent but persistent concerns with and struggles for *independence of action.* The parallel between late adolescence and old-age as settings in which autonomy is a main concern suggests that retirement and the other role losses may open up again the patterns formed in earlier development, perhaps in reverse order.

Meaningful integration refers to the loving, caring, and sharing relationship to one or a very few other persons. It is the opposite of the isolated, mistrustful, resentful and alienated mode of existence now often thought to be characteristic of a great many older people. Integration in this sense is built upon the earlier elements of *compliance* from early childhood, *peer relationships* from later childhood, *acceptance* from early adolescence, *intimacy* from later adolescence, *connection* from young adulthood, *stability* from early maturity, and *dignity* from full maturity. As with all value-themes, it is a human ideal seldom actualized in this imperfect world, but nonetheless powerful in its capacity to provide a standard of comparison and meaning for existing relationships.

Autonomy and integration can at some levels be mutually contradictory, in that extreme individualism toward privatistic goals blocks sharing and caring with others, or in the sense that mutuality and communion may suffocate independence. But where basic values are shared and goals are seen as mutual, integration provides emotional support for autonomy. This combination prevails in some marriages and long-term friendships among the elderly, and could be encouraged by development of the human service role mentioned earlier. When this synthesis of autonomy and integration is achieved, it may go a long way toward making the last years of life maximally rewarding and meaningful. When death does take a member of the

---

[1]   C. Gordon, 'Self-conceptions methodologies', *Journal of Nervous and Mental Disease,* 148 (Spring, 1969), 328-64.

mutual relationship, memory often can preserve the integration. Autonomy then can structure a readiness for one's own death, the drawing of the life-cycle to its final resolution, the final integration.

A CONCLUDING NOTE ON ROLE THEORY AND DEVELOPMENT ACROSS THE LIFE-CYCLE

The role theory perspective used in this chapter was found to be meaningful in interpreting specific findings and low level generalizations concerning role and value development by subsuming them under much more general propositions. In particular, the following propositions from Turner's system (given in Figure 1 of this chapter) were found to be of great usefulness: 1 and 2 setting out the main assumptions concerning role and meaningfulness of human action; 5 on the differential evaluation of roles, 7 on role complementarity and its corollary on adaptiveness; 9 and its corollaries on legitimacy of role expectations; 12 on role-taking; 13 on role adequacy and the corollary on personal evaluation; 14 and its corollaries on role reciprocities; 15 on organizational dominance; 21 on value anchorage; 24 on socialization; and 25 on self-conception development in relation to the adaptiveness and adequacy of role enactment.

In all of these instances, the specific materials at a particular stage or in the transition between stages were significantly illuminated by the reference to the more general and perhaps more familiar pattern of role functioning that had been drawn from more traditional sociological sources dealing with formal organizations and interpersonal interaction.

However, it should be noted that Turner's system does not give sufficient consideration to *role relinquishment.* Investigations into the later portions of the life-cycle make clear what further thought also reveals to be the case even in the early years; life-cycle development involves many instances of either voluntary role relinquishment or undesired, forced role loss. The roles of baby, little kid, punk, teenager, college kid and bachelor or swinger are typical examples of roles given up voluntarily with often only mild and bittersweet regrets. However, the long-term and very strongly institutionalized roles of husband or wife, mother or father, employed person, friend, and healthy person are but a few of the roles that are typically relinquished only with great sadness, pain, and despair. Much more work needs to be done on the typical patterns with which role relinquishment proceeds, and the results of this research should be incorporated within the corpus of role theory as currently formulated.

Finally, additional theoretical and empirical work should be undertaken to trace out the implications of role relinquishment upon major value positions and important self-conceptions. As noted above in connection with review of the research on the post-retirement-age period, the scanty existing evidence suggests at least that as roles are relinquished, behavior, sentiment, motives, interpretation of events, and self-conceptions tend to become disorganized and even painful. In addition to the theoretical importance of investigating the implications of this and further possible generalizations concerning role relinquishment, in human terms the social policy directive is clear. Society must attempt to offer new forms of human service roles that would aid persons of all ages who wish to maintain or increase the cognitive and affective richness of their lives through forms of interaction that offer both the security and the challenge elements that constitute the core meanings of development across the human life-cycle.

5

ROLE: A REDUNDANT CONCEPT
IN SOCIOLOGY? SOME
EDUCATIONAL CONSIDERATIONS[1]

MARGARET A. COULSON

The false idea that 'All the world's a stage and all the men and women merely players' has nevertheless been a compelling one for many sociologists. A number of writers have noted, most with optimism, a few with varying degrees of critical concern, the increase in the use of the concept of role and the development of 'role theory' in recent years. The extent of the increase in 'scholarly output' on role since the 1940s has been documented by Neiman and Hughes, Biddle and Thomas, and Preiss and Ehrlich.[2] Biddle and Thomas, perhaps the most enthusiastic, claim, 'The role analyst may now describe most complex real life phenomena using role terms and concepts, with an exactness which probably surpasses that which is provided by any other single conceptual vocabulary in the behavioural sciences.'[3] Banton, although rather more sceptical of the achievements of role theory is hopeful of its potentialities and suggests, both explicitly and in the organization of his introductory text *Roles,* that most of the main ideas of sociology can be introduced by means of role concepts.[4] Gerth and Mills[5] propose the use of role as a major concept linking character and social structure, but, quite significantly, totally ignore it in the major part of their book. Dahrendorf, in his otherwise critical article, locates '*homo sociologicus,* man as the bearer of socially predetermined roles' at 'the point where individual and society intersect'.[6] Merton claims, quite falsely, that most sociologists would agree that 'social statuses and social roles comprise the major building blocks of social structure'.[7]

1   I should like to thank David Riddell for his assistance with this article.
2   L. J. Neiman and J. W. Hughes, 'The problem of the concept of role – a re-survey of the literature', *Social Forces,* 30 (1951), 141-9; B. J. Biddle and E. H. Thomas (eds.), *Role Theory; Concepts and Research* (New York, 1966); J. Preiss and H. Ehrlich, *An Examination of Role Theory: the Case of the State Police* (Nebraska, 1966).
3   B. J. Biddle and E. H. Thomas, *Role Theory,* p. 9.
4   M. Banton, *Roles* (London, 1965).
5   H. Gerth and C. W. Mills, *Character and Social Structure* (London, 1954).
6   R. Dahrendorf, *Essays in the Theory of Society* (London, 1968).
7   R. Merton, 'The role set: problems in sociological theory', in L. Coser and B. Rosenberg, *Sociological Theory* (London, 1964), pp. 112-22.

These examples illustrate the range and significance of the claims made for the concept of social role. However, the intention of this paper is not simply to comment on the quantity or ambition of such claims. Proponents of role theory have acknowledged some of the inadequacies and confusions of current terminology and usage. But in addition to this, it seems important to consider some of the assumptions in role theory, and their significance for sociology, and to try to explain the sociologists' attachment — or sometimes even commitment — to role theory. It is our contention that one of the main temptations and dangers of sociology is that of what can be termed 'parallelism' — the elaboration of linguistic forms which, with the pretension of explaining the complexity of social reality, merely parallel it in linguistic complexity. The concept of role needs to be looked at with a very sceptical eye. Perhaps it has no significant value whatever apart from its proper theatrical context. In this paper, general criticisms are followed by an examination of a specific area beloved of role theorists — that of the school.

UNDERLYING ASSUMPTIONS IN ROLE THEORY

THE PROBLEM OF DEFINITION

As with other general sociological concepts such as social structure, or the term society itself, there is considerable confusion and ambiguity in the definition of the term 'role'. This confusion enables theorists to use the term in different ways without distinguishing them — or to fall back from one usage to another when under criticism. Surveying the literature in 1951, Neiman and Hughes concluded,

The concept role is at present still rather vague, nebulous, and non-definitive. Frequently the concept is used without any attempt on the part of the writer to define or delimit the concept, the assumption being that both writer and reader will achieve an immediate compatible consensus. Concomitantly, the concept is found frequently in popular usage which adds further confusion.[1]

Where definitions are provided, they often conflict with one another. Biddle and Thomas themselves note, 'The concept of role is the central idea in the language of most role analysts but, ironically, there is probably more disagreement concerning this concept than there is for any other in role theory.'[2] Banton, making the same point, writes, 'What Linton and Newcombe define as role would, in Kingsley Davis' terminology, be a status. What Davis defines as a role, Newcombe calls role behaviour, and T. R. Sarbin, role enactment.'[3] Sometimes role is used to refer to a *social position,* sometimes to the *behaviour* associated with a position — Goffman comments on this: 'It is a position that can be entered, filled and left, not a role, for a role can only be performed; but no student seems to hold to these

1   L. J. Neiman and J. W. Hughes, 'Problem of the concept of role', p. 149.
2   B. J. Biddle and E. H. Thomas, *Role Theory,* p. 29.
3   M. Banton, *Roles,* p. 28.

consistencies, nor will I.'[1] Alternatively role is used to denote *individual* behaviour, or to refer to *typical* behaviour, sometimes in a statistical, sometimes in a normative sense, and so on. But Banton feels able to go on: 'Yet there has been a growing tendency for divergent definitions to be dropped, and a genuine consensus has been achieved which still permits a range of slight variations allowing scope to the interests of writers with different approaches.'[2] Others who express a similar concern about the terminological confusions, nevertheless appear to be committed to the defence of role theory.[3] Gross and his associates suggest that the differences in definitions and vocabulary may be traced to the different disciplines from which the various writers have drawn (anthropology, psychology and sociology) as well as to the differences in the areas of study to which role concepts are applied.[4] A question raised by Neiman and Hughes at the end of their more negatively critical review suggests an alternative explanation: 'Is the concept role, as it is used, an *ad hoc* explanation of human behaviour?'[5] Neiman and Hughes think that the latter view is at least possible.

The authors referred to above have indicated in varying degrees inconsistencies in role language and use. However, there is no consistency in the elements they themselves select as common to other literature. The number of common elements identified varies;[6] Dahrendorf reduces them to two basic aspects — the idea of social position, meaning a place in a field of social relations, and the idea of expected behaviour associated with position, which he himself terms 'role'. But does not reduction of the concept to this level place it totally in question as a useful category? If the essential point is to explore the various expectations which different groups have about the incumbents of particular social positions, then we may be able to approach this more directly if we do *not* introduce the concept of role at all, since it has been a source of much confusion, and has tended to mystify the processes to which it is applied.

THE RELATION OF SOCIETY TO PERSON

At its most general level, role theory implies a sociological view which relates individuals to societies in terms of a process of one-way adjustment and adaptation.

In its crudest forms, this can be seen in many introductory texts in the formulation that 'society' creates roles to which individuals must conform, or that 'society' has needs which men fulfil by playing roles. Berger's *Invitation to Sociology*[7] may be singled out as one of the most misleading books ever written

---

[1] E. Goffman, *Where the Action Is* (London, 1969), p. 39.
[2] M. Banton, *Roles*, p. 28.
[3] J. Preiss and H. Ehrlich, *Examination of Role Theory*; R. Dahrendorf, *Theory of Society*, etc.
[4] N. Gross, W. Mason and A. McEachern, *Exploration in Role Analysis: Studies of the School Superintendency Role* (London, 1966), p. 16.
[5] L. J. Neiman and J. W. Hughes, 'Problem of the concept of role'.
[6] Three for Gross, Mason and McEachern, four for Banton, etc.
[7] P. L. Berger, *Invitation to Sociology* (London, 1966); see especially chs. 4, 5 and 6.

at this level. Time and again, society appears as a mighty 'person', directing and orienting human puppets into their preordained roles. But other writers reveal the same fatal flaw in their conceptualization. For example:

All societies face the functional problem of articulating the components of numerous role-sets, the functional problem of managing somehow to organize these so that an appreciable degree of social regularity obtains, sufficient to enable most people most of the time to go about their business of social life, without encountering extreme conflict in their role sets as the normal, rather than the exceptional, state of affairs.[1]

We are seeking those properties of roles which result from their interrelation in a system within which the requisites of society must be met.

The question as to how far the ritual requisites of society are met by attendance at church or a football match requires lengthy theoretical explanation.[2]

The reification of society illustrated here may in part be due to an effort to emphasize, in the case of text books, the pervasiveness of social influence, perhaps for students whose background orientation may be assumed to be rather individualistic, but such an explanation would hardly hold for the other examples. In no case, however, can the reification be excused, and the misconceptions which stem from this have been adequately outlined by Dahrendorf, who summarizes them thus: 'But who defines social roles, and watches over their acting out? Although many recent writers would answer "society", just as we have so far, the term is hard to justify. *Society is patently not a person, and any personification of it obscures its nature and weakens what is said about it.*'[3]

Associated with this view of society as playwright, devising roles that men must perform, is the implication that there is — or in some way ought to be — consensus about the content of these 'roles'. This is apparent in the way in which the concept is so often introduced: 'People expect appropriate behaviour from the holder of a particular position. The *sum* of these expectations is the role.'[4] 'For the time being it is necessary to assume in the examination of particular roles that there is agreement among all the parties affected as to the definition of the role in question.'[5] Having started with such an assumption (either explicitly or implicitly) there is the problem of how to deal with evidence of dissensus and conflict, and still maintain the theoretical framework and the validity of the concept. Gross and his associates devote a chapter to 'the postulate of role consensus' which has characterized the literature on role,[6] and try to relate it, as with differing definitions of role, to various disciplines or areas of application of the writers concerned. They note that some writers have acknowledged the possibility that role consensus may

---

[1] R. Merton, *Social Theory and Social Structure* (New York, 1957), pp. 377-8.
[2] A. Southall, 'An operational theory of role', *Human Relations,* 12 (1) (1951), 17-34.
[3] R. Dahrendorf, *Theory of Society,* p. 44. My italics.
[4] R. Frankenberg, *Communities in Britain* (London, 1966), pp. 16-17. My italics.
[5] M. Banton, *Roles,* p. 36.
[6] N. Gross, W. Mason and A. McEachern, *Exploration in Role Analysis,* pp. 21ff.

be a variable — or rather that the degree of role consensus may be regarded as variable — for example Parsons and Homans. Banton, quoted above, continues, 'We start with the assumption of consensus but we do not wish to imply that consensus is necessarily found'.[1] However, the question that must be asked is, can discussion of dissensus be legitimately postponed to a later stage? By relegating dissensus in this way, one is encouraged to assume that dissensus is alien to the system, a source of 'disequilibrium', of 'deviance', etc. This is the way the concept is used by Parsons, and also by Merton, as the quotation above indicates.[2] More confused writers have applied the notion of deviant roles very widely, so that even lorry-drivers may be characterized as deviant role players.[3]

Another result of the reification of the society—person relationship is a tendency to conceive existing patterns of behaviour associated in the mind of the author with particular social positions as inevitable, so that, in Parsons' view, the 'domestic' role of middle-class American women and their exclusion from the occupational and instrumental sectors appears to be their necessary contribution to the maintenance and efficiency of the 'system'.[4]

There is no doubt that the general orientation of role theorists is one of social determinism. Their view of man is that of a creature moulded by society in a process which is unidirectional. Their view of society assumes a highly integrated subsystem. That such an orientation is implied is recognized in various ways. Goffman argues:

In entering the position, the incumbent finds that he must take on the whole array of action encompassed by the corresponding role, so role implies a social determinism and a doctrine about socialization. Role then is the basic element of socialization. It is through roles that tasks in society are allocated and arrangements made to enforce their performance.[5]

It is interesting that Goffman's actual work employs role with greater flexibility and modification than such general statements as this lead one to expect. Preiss and Ehrlich consider that role theory is 'an essentially deterministic theory', and that as such it is best suited to 'highly structured social systems where the goals of those systems are well elaborated . . . We do not think that role theory can handle adequately expressive social systems, matters of primary group relations or transitory collective behavioural phenomena'.[6] That is, they reject the validity

1 M. Banton, *Roles*, p. 36.
2 Compare T. Parsons, *The Social System* (Glencoe, Ill., 1951) and R. Merton, 'The role set: problems in sociological theory'.
3 See P. Musgrave, 'Towards a sociological theory of occupational choice', *Sociological Review*, 15 (1967), 33-46, criticized in M. Coulson, T. Keil, D. Riddell and S. Struthers, 'Towards a theory of occupational choice — a critique', *Sociological Review*, 15 (1967), 301-9.
4 T. Parsons, 'Age and sex in the social structure of the United States', *American Sociological Review*, 7 (1942), 604-16.
5 E. Goffman, *Where the Action Is*, p. 41.
6 J. Preiss and H. Ehrlich, *An Examination of Role Theory*, p. 168.

of the application of role concepts to family relationships, and other supposedly 'expressive social systems' of which a considerable number are listed in their bibliography. Dahrendorf points to the unreality and dangers of a model of man as role conformer. However, he argues that sociologists are concerned with an artificial construct which has value for sociological theory, and not with a philosophical statement about man, and it is their duty to make the difference clear to non-sociologists. But even were we to accept this quite arbitrary distinction, the artificial construct for which this kind of role theory has relevance was rather effectively demolished by Dahrendorf himself some years previously. Utopias have some attractions after all, as many liberal politicians have come to recognize.[1]

Wrong's discussion of the limitations implicit in such an oversocialized conception of man is of relevance here. He points out that the process of socialization may be understood in two ways — 'On the one hand as the transmission of culture, the particular culture an individual enters at birth; on the other hand the term is used to mean the process of becoming human, of acquiring uniquely human attributes from *interaction* with others'. Socialization in this latter meaning is left out of role theory, and this is because it does not fit into the scheme of society as an integrated system on which the theory depends. 'When our sociological theory overstresses the stability and integration of society we will end up imagining that man is the disembodied, conscience driven, status-seeking phantom of current theory.'[2]

THE APPEAL OF THE CONCEPT OF ROLE TO SOCIOLOGISTS

The material presented so far is intended to illustrate the confusion of role theorists themselves and the inadequacy of their approach. Yet why should such a dubious concept have such a wide appeal? Of course, the idea of men as role players comes from the theatre, and role theory is developed out of an analogy between social life and the stage. The appeal of this analogy is that at its simplest level it provides a way of emphasizing the influence and pervasiveness of social forces which is readily understood, and which may appear to be very useful at an introductory stage (for example Berger's use of the analogy, referred to earlier). The apparent aptness of the idea of role playing may be reinforced for the sociologists by their own social experience. As academics, as teachers, as members of the professional middle class, perhaps upwardly socially mobile, they may feel that much of social life consists of acting, of creating impressions of intellectual merit, of extensive knowledge, of authority and reliability in the eyes of their students, their colleagues, their superiors in the academic heirarchy; the formal lecture may appear similar to a theatrical performance — though not necessarily to the student audience; for some

1   R. Dahrendorf, *Theory of Society*.
2   D. Wrong, 'The oversocialized conception of man in modern sociology', in L. Coser and B. Rosenberg, *Sociological Theory* (London, 1964), pp. 112-22.

there may be an awareness of regulating their behaviour to fit a part defined for them by others with more power or authority, as for example, the self-censorship reported by many American social scientists in Lazarsfeld's enquiry.[1]

From the sociologist's own social situation, then, the ideas of role theory may have a direct appeal which is readily assumed to extend to social life generally; everyone really is acting all the time. In addition, as already noted, role theory is a part of, and is totally consistent with, the functionalist orientation in sociology, which has been a predominant one in the United States and to a lesser extent in Britain in the post-war period.

Like other analogies which have become part of some sociology (for example, organic and mechanical analogies) the idea of social life as drama can and often has been carried so far that the analogy becomes more real to the author than the social actions and interactions which it is supposed to represent. Besides this, the recognition of social role as part of an analogy is quickly forgotten by some writers, and the concept becomes part of a complicated theoretical construction which to its authors seems to acquire an overriding significance and meaning of its own. Theory building of this style is, perhaps, one of the methods by which sociologists attempt to establish sociology in the academic tradition. Let us use Biddle and Thomas to exemplify the delights of abstraction, while some of the work of Goffman illustrates those of the frustrated dramatist.

Biddle and Thomas present *Role Theory: Concepts and Research* as an authoritative statement and development of role theory for which they make relatively ambitious claims, already referred to above. Their book consists of a selection of articles and extracts from various writers, in which role concepts are used. This is preceded by a section on the background and theoretical structure of role theory which is supposedly directed towards a *clarification* of the language and theoretical formulations of role theory. Biddle and Thomas reject Linton's association of role with status (or position) as too limiting; their more extensive aim is to 'encompass the numerous and subtle ways in which persons may be associated with behaviours. To handle systematically these relationships, we shall define and discuss a person—behaviour matrix that deals with the interface between persons and behaviour'.[2] This explanation itself is precisely as clear as the word 'interface' upon which it depends. Once set upon course, the authors' concept building becomes increasingly elaborate and increasingly divorced from 'the real life behaviour as it is displayed in ongoing social situations' which it is supposed to be capable of illuminating. The following extract would not disgrace Parsons at his worst:

Concepts for Person—Behaviour Segments. Concepts within the person—behaviour segment combine particularizations from both the person set and the behavioural region set. For instance, we may easily distinguish the *overt behaviour role* from the

1   This idea is developed somewhat in M. Coulson and D. Riddell, *Approaching Sociology* (London, 1970).
2   B. J. Biddle and E. H. Thomas, *Role Theory,* p. 29.

overt target role, and both of these from the *covert-prescriptive role,* and so forth. Other, more specialized, person–behaviour roles also appear in the literature. One of these centers on the term 'characteristic'. Roles are sometimes defined as those patterns of behaviour characteristic of certain persons. The idea of 'characteristic' is that the behaviours referenced *are* performed by the persons designated – and often. Thus, it is characteristic for policemen to stand on corners and direct traffic. In order to isolate a *characteristic role,* one would have to sort through the person segment for those individuals designated to find out which behaviours were frequently emitted. (See Ch. IV for an additional discussion of this concept under *behavioural commonality.*) A *unique role* would be a characteristic role found only for those persons designated.

And as postscript to this section:

It is impossible to capture the diversity and complexity of the person–behaviour matrix with a single concept such as role. The specific referents for the segments relating to persons, to behaviour, and to persons and behaviour call for scores of concepts and identifying terms, as the prior discussion demonstrates. Because the single idea of role is inarticulate in the face of such complexity, the question naturally arises as to whether the word 'role' should be abandoned altogether. We think not, provided that the word is employed only by itself to denote the generic idea of the particular behaviour of given persons, i.e. to refer to the entire person–behaviour matrix, and provided that more specific concepts are used when speaking of given segments of the matrix.[1]

And thus the need for ever more complicated qualifications, and sub-qualifications is established, while the relationship of the theory to the policeman's actual behaviour, for example, becomes ever more remote and unconvincing. If the single concept of role is inarticulate in face of the complexities of social behaviour (and in this we are agreed), it is interesting that the wordy edifice constructed upon this inadequate concept is expected to provide an *articulate* conceptual framework for understanding social behaviour. To *parallel* the complexities of the social world by devising complicated theoretical formulations may be an absorbing, if irrelevant, intellectual exercise, but explanation and prediction of behaviour cannot be expected to result from it.

The work of Erving Goffman provides a contrast to the arid abstractions of Biddle and Thomas. Goffman's theorizing is always related to acute observations of human behaviour, and the main concern is to explore in a dialectical way the interactions of individuals in the social situations in which they find themselves. He makes frequent use of analogies in his work; social life is seen as a game, as a drama, and so on. Despite the frequent use of theatrical analogy, Goffman's actual use of the term role has not been extensive; indeed in *The Presentation of Self* and *Asylums* it is rarely employed.[2] Often the analogies and concepts deriving from

---

1   *Ibid.* p. 31.
2   E. Goffman, *The Presentation of Self in Everyday Life* (New York, 1959); E. Goffman, *Asylums* (London, 1968).

them are used to throw light on quite specific, clearly limited and defined situations; in the article on Role Distance, in which an attempt is made to consider and broaden the concept of social role, the examples are taken from observations of the operating theatre and the merry-go-round.[1] Via the concept of role distance the ways and extent to which individuals distance themselves from the expectations which attach to their positions in particular social situations are explored, and vividly illustrated by the observations of the behaviour of older children and adults on a merry-go-round. While Goffman's paper does not − in this author's view − avoid many of the shortcomings of role theory, his concept of role distance is a serious attempt 'to combat this tendency to keep a part of the world safe from sociology',[2] to bridge one of the gaps between observable social behaviour and 'role theory'. Goffman's application of role concepts is to what he calls 'close studies of moment to moment behaviour'. Partly because of this and partly because of the imaginative use of analogies, and the perceptiveness of the examples, some of the weaknesses of role theory appear less obviously here. Yet they are not avoided. Thus society is reified: 'The individual limits the degree to which he embraces a situated role, or is required to embrace it, because of *society's understanding* of him as a multiple role performer rather than as a person with a particular role.'[3] And so, according to Goffman, as multiple role players both the business executive and the soldier are permitted time away from work when their wives are having a baby; but the lack of any wider social structural perspective and the reification of society prevent any analysis of the variation in the *extent* to which individuals in different occupational positions are expected to compartmentalize their lives. 'Society' is not able to 'recognize' in any way that its members are all 'multiple role players', and such a formulation makes impossible further examination of the actual way in which different groups of people relate to each other in specific societies and the processes by which such relationships emerge.

The theatrical analogy from which role theory has been developed is an attractive one, and Goffman's usage is more perceptive than most. However, as with all analogies, unless the differences, as well as the similarities, with social phenomena are clearly and carefully outlined, the concepts which are developed will be misleading ones.

CONFLICT AND INDIVIDUAL; MAJOR PROBLEMS FOR ROLE ANALYSIS

When the role analogy is applied to social life, two major 'problems' are encountered. Firstly, that of how to incorporate any *lack of consensus* among different people in their expectations of the holder of a particular position; secondly, how to deal with the *individuals* who fill these positions. If all the

[1] E. Goffman, *Where the Action Is.*
[2] *Ibid.* p. 103.
[3] *Ibid.* p. 94. My italics.

world really were a stage and all the men and women merely players, then role
theory would provide us with just the conceptual framework necessary for
understanding, although even in a play directors and actors and critics may come
into conflict as to the author's intentions. The world however is not a stage. How
have role theorists met this fact — apart, of course, from the considerable number
who have chosen to ignore it? Merton's use of role conflict and role set, Gross,
Mason and McEachern's segmentation of position and role, and Dahrendorf's
development of their ideas are among the more serious attempts to recognize
conflicting expectations. The same writers' conceptions of the persons who fill
the positions and 'play' roles will be considered.

Merton has recognized that differing and sometimes conflicting expectations of
the incumbent of a 'status position' may be held by different members of his 'role
set' and that these differences may be associated with differences in the social
positions of different 'role set' members. Various mechanisms operate to control
the degree of role conflict. The power and authority of role set members varies
considerably, as does the extent to which they are able to observe how the role
player actually performs his part; they may be ignorant of the differences in their
expectations, and if they become aware of them, the conflict may develop as one
between the role set members leaving the central 'status position' holder as observer.
However, Merton does not explain the ways in which power relationships may
change and the extent to which a position holder may nevertheless be influenced
by those who *cannot* directly observe what he does. But the basic underlying
limitation is the implication that conflict should not be there, that conflicting
expectations are an interruption — albeit one which is commonly found — in the
efficiency of the role system.

Even when these mechanisms are operating, they may not, in particular cases, prove
sufficient to reduce the conflict of expectations below the level required for the
social structure to operate with substantial effectiveness. This residual conflict
within the role set may be enough to interfere materially with the *effective*
performance of roles by the occupant of the status in question.[1]

We are faced with the problem of what constitutes efficiency. It is a small step from
this to the reification of society, to notions of the 'national interest', the needs of
the system and so on. Let us look at this problem through an example.

In the administration of British technical colleges, the keeping of rather elaborate
class registers is an activity to which considerable importance is attached, involving
work for clerical, administrative and teaching staff. Teaching staff who keep
immaculate registers may be highly regarded by college administrators, while those
who treat this activity with contempt, or pay little regard to accuracy and neatness
may be heavily criticized, even where large numbers of the students of the former
group fail their examinations or don't complete their courses, while relatively high

1   R. Merton, 'The role set . . .', p. 385. My italics.

proportions of the students of the latter group are successful (such a relationship does not, of course, necessarily apply). Here is a situation of conflicting expectations about college lecturers, in which the views of their responsibilities held by the lecturers as well as other 'role set' members must be included. But the conflict cannot be explained as an intrusion into the system which upsets its (undefined) efficiency, for it derives from the structure of the college system itself, and from the differing and conflicting historical and contemporary expectations about technical education in our society.

Gross, Mason and McEachern make the most systematic attempt to examine the 'postulate of role consensus', and they conclude the chapter devoted to this:

In contrast to the holistic approach so frequently found in social science literature, that is, that a role is an indivisible *unit* of rights and obligations ascribed by a group or society, theoretically grounded empirical enquiries are needed to determine how much agreement there is on the expectations for behaviour of position incumbents. Conceptual schemes for role analysis that preclude the investigation of basic questions of role consensus are distinctly limited.[1]

And, one should add, misleading. Yet in setting up a 'Language for Role Analysis',[2] role is defined as 'a set of expectations, or in terms of our definition of expectations, it is a set of evaluative standards applied to the incumbent of a particular position'.[3] So that role itself, without the assumption of consensus becomes an unstructured concept of somewhat limited and questionable descriptive value. In their research into the expectations which various groups — teachers, principals, school board members, school superintendents themselves — had of school superintendents, Gross and his colleagues found a wide range of variations and conflicts. They maintain their commitment to role theory by segmenting position and role so that a *focal position* (school superintendent) faces a series of *counter positions* (teachers, other superintendents, school board members, etc.) and the set of expectations which each different counter position holds is termed the *role sector*. But in interpreting their research finding, Gross and colleagues suggest that the school superintendency role can be defined in terms of the distribution of responses to their questionnaires, thus revealing a totally inadequate evaluation of the *structure* of relationships between incumbents of various counter positions and with the focal position. Dahrendorf makes this criticism:

By attributing the force of social norms to the uncertain basis of majority opinions, he makes the fact of society subject to the arbitrariness of questionnaire responses. If six out of ten parents interviewed think that a school superintendent should not smoke and should be married, these expected attributes or actions are for Gross constituents of the role of school superintendent; if, on the other hand — Gross does not go thus far, but nothing in his approach rules out such absurdities — 35

1 N. Gross, W. Mason and A. McEachern, *Exploration in Role Analysis*, p. 43.
2 *Ibid.* ch. 4, pp. 48ff.
3 *Ibid.* p. 61.

out of 40 pupils think that none of them should ever get bad marks, this too is an expectation, associated in the first instance with the role of teacher, but applying also to the school superintendent as the teacher's superior.[1]

A more crude example of this type of error may be found in Preiss and Ehrlich's study of the state police. In their research, they asked policemen about how they perceived the expectations which eleven audience groups had of them. In discussing the responses, they write, 'We shall arbitrarily label the *numerically smaller* expectation the "conflict-producing" response, and the audience perceived as holding this expectation as the "deviant audience".'[2] With such a supposedly arbitrary choice of labels the most misleading theories may be devised, and the close attachment of role theory to a consensus model of society may be illustrated.

Dahrendorf, nevertheless, develops the ideas of Gross, Mason and McEachern, introducing the concept of reference groups linked to every social position. So, 'to articulate expectations for a given position, we must first identify the position's reference groups and then find what norms obtain in these groups with respect to that particular position'.[3] He differentiates three types of expectations: *must* expectations which operate at the societal level and are enforced by law; *shall* expectations which may derive from various types of public organization, professional associations, political parties, etc., etc., which may define, with varying degrees of authority, norms and sanctions; *can* expectations which are uncodified, informal expectations not to be confused with the opinions which can be elicited in what Dahrendorf aptly calls 'the behavioural pseudo-science of opinion research'.

Dahrendorf's essay 'Homo Sociologicus' rejects the assumption of consensus and provides some conception of a structured relationship between a social position and the reference groups with which it is associated. Such a framework enables us to examine sets of expectations about the incumbent of that social position. In a more peripheral way, the potentially changing nature of expectations is recognized. And yet, as the theory becomes more adequate to the explanation of social life, the reason for pinning it to the concept of role becomes more obscure. And Dahrendorf's own definitions of the concept are as restricted and unstructured as those of Gross: 'Roles are bundles of expectations directed at the incumbents of positions in a given society', or roles are 'complexes of behaviour expectations adhering to social positions'.[4] Although Dahrendorf considers that role is a more important concept than position, it is not clear that the notion of a 'bundle of expectations' is analytically useful, for if we wish to develop, or to apply the concept, we at once have − to continue the metaphor − to untie the bundle, and to trace back the relationships between positions and expectations which have been lumped together within it.

[1] R. Dahrendorf, *Theory of Society*, p. 48.
[2] J. Preiss and H. Ehrlich, *Examination of Role Theory*, pp. 107-8. My italics.
[3] R. Dahrendorf, *Theory of Society*, p. 49.
[4] *Ibid.* p. 36, p. 73.

If role theory collapses without the assumption of agreement about expectations, it is equally incoherent in the face of the individuals who supposedly play the roles. By their reliance on an understanding of the process of socialization as a one-way adaptation of individual to society, role theorists have been able to ignore the dimension of the individual's process of social learning and his biography. Thus Merton underplays the possibilities of individual variation in role conflict, by leaving out the variable of individual life history, and emphasizing that any conflict of expectations among members of a role set will be more or less commonly experienced by all the occupants of a particular social position.[1] Gross, Mason and McEachern direct their *Explorations in Role Analysis* to 'studies of the school *superintendency* role'. The very title implies an abstraction above the level of the school superintendents concerned. In his critical review of this work, Naegele writes,

I think the methods of this book, for all the richness of particular regularities that they yielded, dissolve rather than explain, the phenomena they seek to unravel. Even half alive men cohere and have some sort of centre. An exploration unhaunted by this fact produces a false and incomplete image, falsely completed in the imagination of us, the readers. Nor is this a humanistic or clinical plea against abstraction. Quite the contrary, it is a plea for appropriate abstraction.[2]

This last point is the important one. To argue that the individual is the concern of psychology or philosophy and not of sociology is to miss the point. Sociological theory does not have to be reduced to individual psychology — nor to claim to take over from philosophy — in order to make allowance for human individuality; no adequate sociological theory can avoid this variable. Theoretical concepts which can be used to describe, explain and eventually predict social phenomena are, of course, artificial constructs, as Dahrendorf argues. But this does not mean that they must be defended when they seriously distort the social phenomena which they seek to represent. The concept of role, with its reliance on a view of man as role conformer and of society as integrated role system is such a distortion. It is time that these inadequacies were recognized and that the concept of role was abandoned by sociologists. *Without it* we are able to examine the relationships between the expectations which members of different groups hold of the incumbents of a particular social position in a more flexible and dynamic way, one in which the structure of relationships existing and developing between the different groups in turn structures the expectations, and their consequences for the behaviour of the position holder are understood as part of an interaction with the individual's own learned expectations. The process is thus a dialectical one and presupposes neither unified sets of expectations about people in different positions, nor a passive individual adaptation to such sets of expectations.

1   R. Merton, *Social Theory and Social Structure*, p. 383.
2   K. D. Naegele, 'Superintendency versus superintendents: a critical essay', *Harvard Educational Review*, 30 (1960), 372-93.

ROLES OR EXPECTATIONS? (A framework for understanding social
interactions in schools)

The introduction in Britain of sociology into teacher-training courses has largely
been a development of the 1960s. As well as the quite extensive documentation of
the relationship between education and social class over the past twenty years, the
sociology of education as a subject has expanded rapidly during the period, and a
considerable number of introductory texts and small studies have appeared recently.
The orientation of these latter has been overwhelmingly functionalist, strongly
influenced by Durkheim and by Parsons, and is thus to some extent in accord with
the dominant culture of the colleges of education, at least as that has been
interpreted by Taylor:

The stress upon the interpersonal, the intuitive and the intangible, the community
and the group, the criticisms of 'culture' rather than structure are all such as to
strengthen the teachers' capacity for socializing the child within a framework of
social attributes and assumptions that value cohesion rather than conflict, loyalty
rather than engagement, stability rather than change.[1]

Within such a context, and within such a functionalist theoretical orientation,
the ideas of role theory have readily taken their place; some examples will be
examined below.

TEACHERS AS ACTORS

The theatrical analogy has had its particular attractions for educational sociologists
and others interested and involved in education. Westwood has provided a general
summary of much of this work.[2] There is a popular idea that teachers cannot 'be
themselves' in their relationships with pupils; they must put on an act. This idea
may be considerably reinforced by much that is taught in colleges of education with
reference to teaching practice, and in many cases by what is experienced in schools
by students and beginning teachers. It has received some theoretical legitimation
from the writings of educational sociologists ever since William Waller's emphasis
that the teacher's maintenance of social distance from the pupils is important for
effective teaching. However, such formulations allow for only *one* particular type
of teacher—pupil relationship (even though this may often have taken on the
appearance of *the* inevitable type). But work in schools such as Summerhill,
developments in junior school teaching as for example current work in some
Oxfordshire junior schools, the demands for a more democratic education now
made by some students in schools and universities, all indicate that other models

1 W. Taylor, *Society and the Education of Teachers* (London, 1969), p. 286.
2 L. J. Westwood, 'The role of the teacher I', *Educational Research*, 9, no. 2 (February 1967),
   122-34; 'The role of the teacher II', *Educational Research*, 10, no. 1 (November 1967),
   21-37. In these articles Westwood raises many criticisms of role theory in the field of
   education. However his criticisms are somewhat uncertain and incomplete, and finally
   evaporate in a conclusion that the attempt to apply role concepts is nevertheless worthwhile.

of teaching/learning are actually available, and thus no adequate theoretical framework can exclude them.

TEACHERS AND PUPILS IN THE ONE-WAY ADAPTATION OF INDIVIDUALS TO SOCIETY

Talcott Parsons' article *The School Class as a Social System* has had an inordinate influence on the writings of educational sociologists. In it, Parsons discusses the problems, 'first of how the school class functions to internalize in its pupils both the commitments and capacities for successful performance of their future adult roles, and second of how it functions to allocate these human resources within the role structure of the adult society'.[1] Thus a framework is set up for the study of education as a one-way process of adaptation and allocation in which pupils are moulded to fit their particular future parts. Kelsall and Kelsall have translated Parson's article into a definition of the 'teacher's role' in a chapter significantly entitled, 'The role that society is assumed to want its teachers to fulfil'.[2] Who makes the assumptions? Who holds such ideas of the 'teacher's role'? Blyth, in his sociological description of English primary education, relies heavily on the same article; he notes for example, 'As Talcott Parsons points out, the good pupil role involves achievement in both instruction and socialization'.[3] Thus, the 'good pupil role' is apparently defined solely by the teacher, and the *interplay* of social and academic factors in the teacher's assessment of 'good pupils' cannot be explored in such a formulation. The teacher's 'ascribed roles' are listed as those of instructor, parent-substitute, organizer, value-bearer, classifier, welfare worker, thus paralleling four of the five 'roles of the school' which Blyth suggests earlier. The formulation, as the title of the book implies, is descriptive. Why these descriptions rather than others is not explicitly stated, but cannot be detached from the functionalist basis of the study. There are many other examples of the difficulties which arise from such an orientation. For example Musgrave has suggested that the 'teacher's role' has two main aspects, 'the self image' of the teacher and the 'public image'. This oversimplification in combination with the assumption of a unitary 'social system' leads to the following conclusion:

The teacher who begins his career with the soundest possible of motives may in time change so that he is no longer helping the children as much as he might. This conclusion emphasizes the need for continual self-assessment by practising teachers to see whether their idea of what they are doing meets the public need. If it does not, the teacher is not having the maximum possible effect on the children.[4]

1 T. Parsons, 'The school class as a social system: some of its functions in American society', in J. Floud, A. H. Halsey and C. Anderson, *Education, Economy and Society* (Glencoe, Ill., 1961).
2 R. K. Kelsall and H. M. Kelsall, *The School Teacher in England and the United States* (London, 1969), p. 14.
3 W. A. C. Blyth, *English Primary Education: A Sociological Description* (London, 1968), vol. 1, p. 93.
4 P. Musgrave, *The Sociology of Education* (London, 1965), p. 270.

E

'The public need' is not defined, as, it is argued, this is a matter for philosophy, not sociology; nevertheless the implication is clear, in order to play his part properly the teacher *must* adapt his behaviour to meet 'its' requirements. The alternatives appear to be conformity or deviance. Elsewhere Musgrave has recognized that the teacher's 'role' 'changes through time', and also that 'to speak of the role of the teacher in any unitary way is over simple'.[1] But as the general theoretical assumptions remain the same these characteristics can only be treated as 'problems' (both for the sociologist and for 'the system'?). Shipman has created similar problems for similar reasons.[2] But how, if tied to such assumptions, could we explain sociologically the conflicts which led to the closing of Risinghill Comprehensive school, or which have emerged recently at Warwick University or which, in an American context are dramatized in Kozol's description of, and involvement in, the school situation of black children in Boston.[3] A sociology which has to treat such situations as 'exceptions' as 'imbalances' as 'deviations' — as role theory does — is indeed feeble.

TEACHER'S ROLE – THE SUM OF OTHER PEOPLE'S EXPECTATIONS?

Musgrove and Taylor's recent study *Society and the Teacher's Role,* can provide an example for discussion here to which other work can be related. The study is presented as a small-scale empirical inquiry into the teacher's role in contemporary Britain: 'The book reports the way teachers see their job, the way they think other people significantly related to their job see it, and the way these people (particularly parents and pupils) do in fact see it.'[4] The research therefore follows what is becoming a major empirical method of role theorists in sociology — a comparison of the responses of various groups to questions or statements about the expectations they have for the holders of a particular social position (in this case school teachers), with the reported perceptions of those expectations held by teachers themselves, and the teachers' own perceptions of their actual behaviour. Further levels of comparison may be added by asking for the view which each group has of the expectations of every other group and so on. From such responses, the appropriate role is somehow computed.[5]

Like these other investigators, Musgrove and Taylor find that teachers report 'inaccurate' perceptions of the expectations which other groups hold of them.

---

1   P. Musgrave, *The School as a Social Organization* (London, 1968), p. 64, p. 66.
2   M. D. Shipman, *The Sociology of the School* (London, 1968).
3   J. Kozol, *Death at an Early Age* (London, 1968).
4   F. Musgrove, P. Taylor, *Society and the Teacher's Role* (London, 1969), p. 8.
5   For other examples of similar methods see B. J. Biddle, H. A. Rosencranz and E. F. Rankin, *Studies in the Role of the Public School Teacher* (Milwaukee, 1961); N. Gross, W. Mason and A. McEachern, *Exploration in Role Analysis*; J. Preiss and H. Ehrlich, *Examination of Role Theory*.

They summarize thus:

Teachers in all types of school saw their work primarily in intellectual and moral terms, placing great weight on instruction in subjects and moral training. They placed relatively little emphasis on social objectives in general and least of all on 'social advancement' in particular. In no type of school were teachers prepared to see themselves primarily as agents of social mobility. They saw parents as being comparatively indifferent to moral and social training, but placing great weight on instruction and social advancement. In fact parents in general emphasized the same objectives as teachers: moral training and instruction in subjects, and like teachers, gave comparatively little weight to 'social advancement'.[1]

What does this approach and these findings tell us about the pressures which influence the processes of interaction between teachers and pupils within schools? That there is quite an extensive distaste for what goes on? That is not Musgrove and Taylor's conclusion, but it is difficult to draw much else from their work. No investigation can do more than its research method allows. The rank ordering of general educational aims can only tell us about the abstract preferences of teachers, pupils and parents in questionnaire responses. And the conclusion of Musgrove and Taylor that, for the teachers, 'the area of (unnecessary) tension might be considerably reduced if parents and teachers established some effective means of communication', emphasizes the extent to which the factors which structure the relationships between these groups can be ignored.

One of the perhaps unintended contributions of empirical research by role theorists has been to show that many people are unable to predict accurately how other specified groups will define, in questionnaire responses, their expectations about those in a given social position, including how the position holders concerned see themselves. Biddle and associates report a complex of misconceptions held by teachers, parents, pupils and school officials about the expectations which each group held for school teachers in Kansas City. Most groups underestimated the 'liberalism' of others' expectations; teachers, parents and pupils expected school officials to hold more authoritarian views than they in fact expressed. Teachers' views were much closer to those of school officials than the teachers recognized; parents claimed attitudes which were less 'conservative' than teachers or school officials anticipated. From this, Biddle and his associates are led to wonder

what would happen if school officials were apprised that public opinion was generally more liberal than they gave credit for; or a serious attempt was made by the school system to sample public opinion regarding teacher role on a regular basis. It is possible that changes might be wrought for the role of teacher, and that the professions of teacher and school administrator might become more attractive.[2]

[1] F. Musgrove and P. Taylor, *The Teacher's Role*, p. 63.
[2] B. J. Biddle and E. H. Thomas, *Role Theory*, p. 309.

So the main problems are problems of communication, and frequent opinion-polls might resolve the confusion and ambiguity of the 'teacher's role' — *and thereby even attract more teachers!* However, another finding that Musgrove and Taylor draw from their investigation is that in the opinion of pupils, 'The good teacher is a young married man with children who gives little homework and no corporal punishment'.[1] It is hard to see how the regular collection of such opinions could contribute to an increase in recruits for the profession! The opinion pollster's view of social processes, already criticized in the preceding sections, is perfectly captured here. How from such an approach would one predict that the discontents of teachers would reach such an intensity that they would strike, closing and partially closing schools in many areas? Or what the various responses to such action might be? (England and Wales and Scotland in the 1969–70 academic year.)

AN ALTERNATIVE APPROACH

These examples merely re-emphasize the inadequacies and misconceptions of 'role analysis' already outlined in general. Where can we find a more adequate and dynamic perspective? A short paper by Webb seems to offer a potentially more adequate approach than all the endeavours of the role theorists together.[2] In this Webb sketches a framework for examining social relationships in a slum secondary modern school, 'Black School'.[3] Hostility characterizes relationships between boys and teachers. The 'drill-sergeant' methods of the teachers and the active or passive 'guerrilla-war' activity of the pupils against them are explained with reference to the other groups to which each is related and responsive. The teacher immediately confronts his class, but the expectations of other teachers and of the head teacher are always close at hand. To be well regarded by these latter it is necessary to maintain control, to minimize noise. Drill-sergeant teaching appears to do this and can be justified by the staff ideology which itself provides some protection against external pressures. Besides, the boys take advantage of any teacher who tries a more humane technique; outside school they are members of street gangs and destined for routine, semi-skilled jobs. Their spontaneity and irresponsibility are reinforced in gang activities, while the authoritarianism of the school helps them to focus the gang's opposition to 'them' more sharply. These same characteristics will be a major defence for them against the tedium of their future work. The head teacher's absorption in administrative tasks, his tremendous enthusiasm for some minor achievement when talking to the HMI, and the Inspector's exaggeration of that exaggeration, help to insulate the school against external criticism.

Clearly this is the beginning of a framework only, implied by description rather

---

1   F. Musgrove and P. Taylor, *The Teacher's Role*, p. 26.
2   J. Webb, 'The sociology of a school', *British Journal of Sociology*, 13, no. 3, pp. 264-72.
3   D. H. Hargreaves, *Social Relations in a Secondary School* (London, 1967), and J. Partridge, *Life in a Secondary Modern School* (London, 1968) have provided some documentation of schools which in some degree approximate to the model of Black School.

than conceptualized. There is no consideration of individual variations, and the location of the school within the educational and wider social structure is only partially acknowledged. But there is a recognition that teachers are themselves not in a position to choose the organization and processes within the school. Compare this with Musgrove and Taylor's amazing notion that teachers are a 'self-styled corps d'élite which decides what kinds of creatures its children shall be, their life styles, their life chances'.[1] It must be admitted that this misguided view probably derives not only from the role framework, but must be closely associated with the conclusion which follows it — that only when a free choice between different types of education is available to parents will teachers be controlled by a proper contractual relationship to their clients (parents!), comparable to other professional groups.

Webb directs our attention to the process of interaction between what is expected by one group and by another, the relationship between what is learned in one group and in another, the relationship between what goes on within the school and the social world outside, the shifting basis of power and authority, as determinants of the behaviour of teachers and pupils.

We can try to look at these processes in a more general outline. Teacher and pupils interact within classrooms, the presence of other observers is rare — sometimes a student, in some circumstances an LEA advisor or an HMI. The pupils have the potential power of many against one; the teacher has some authority from her appointment and some power in her responsibility for the 'academic' assessment of her pupils.[2] The extent to which the pupils exercise their power will vary according to such features as their age, sex, social class background, the expectations of their parents, the type of school and its internal organization, their previous school experiences, as well as the behaviour and expectations of their present teacher. Their expectations of her will vary with these factors too, and will not, of course, be uniform for all members of a class; and the same factors may be expected to modify the teacher's behaviour towards, and expectations of, her pupils. The teacher's own biography, her age, her own educational experience and training (if any), her status in the school, the subject or age group she teaches, the expectations of other teachers, of the head teacher, and of the educational administrators, inspectors and advisers behind him, may in varying degrees, directly or indirectly comprise influences on her behaviour in the class-room. The effectiveness of her authority, and the extent to which she emphasizes it or minimizes it in her relationships with pupils will depend largely on the particular combination of these factors.

1 F. Musgrove and P. Taylor, *The Teacher's Role*, p. 85.
2 The teacher is not of course necessarily female. The use of the feminine pronoun is intended neither to imply an exclusion of male teachers, nor to direct attention to primary rather than secondary education. However a majority of school teachers *are* women, and any very general statement about the social position of school teachers cannot ignore this — not insignificant — fact.

So far we have only a list of some of the groups and situations, and not a comprehensive one at that. To go further, we have to be able to *structure* the relationships between the various reference groups which have been mentioned, and this requires some conception of the structure of the educational system and of its relation to the structure of the society, which gives us the principles of the structuring. Only by emphasizing this wider framework can we avoid the tendency to give the strongest weight to expectations held by a numerical majority, and so become able to examine, in a coherent way, the range and development of power and authority relationships, the limits of sanctions which can be imposed by one group on another, the extent of the influence which those who are currently out of sight may still exert.

Teachers in Britain work within an educational system which is traditionally individualistic and competitive, in which pupils are constantly ranked and assessed against one another, within an hierarchical system of examinations and institutions. For the pupils, success within this competitive structure may provide significant means of social advancement. The history of the extension and development of state education in Britain has been such as to link it closely to the structure of economic and social opportunities. Nineteenth-century economic developments, the development of new industrial processes and techniques were a major impetus to the establishment of universal state education, just as the expansion and changes in higher education today owe, to a significant extent, their initiation to more recent economic factors.[1] But the general structure of the education system provides personnel for a stratified occupational structure.[2]

The hierarchy of schools is compounded by the hierarchy of social backgrounds of their pupils, involving not only cultural differences between working-class and middle-class children, but also, often, material differences in educational provision — the tendency for poor schools to be located in poor neighbourhoods which was recognized by both the Newsom and Plowden Reports. In post-1944 developments, secondary modern schools were offered as an 'equal but different' form of secondary education; a formulation which not only disregarded the very unequal social chances following from education within them, but also their unequal right to resources as reflected in the Burnham allocations. Such factors cannot be set on one side by anyone attempting to understand what goes on within such schools, and they are essential to the understanding of what teachers do when they teach.

As has been stressed above, there are many methods of teaching, and teacher–pupil relationships corresponding to them. Nevertheless, the competitive cultural demands of a competitive social structure, have led teaching to become centrally

---

1 This is not to suggest that economic factors are the sole determinants — see, for example, P. Simon, *Education and the Labour Movement* (London, 1965) and E. P. Thompson, *Warwick University, Ltd.* (London, 1970).

2 For a brilliant elaboration of this theme for France see P. Bordieu, 'Cultural reproduction and social reproduction' (Paper read at the British Sociological Association Conference, Spring 1970).

involved in testing, examining, evaluating, predicting the attainments of pupils, formally through tests of 'intelligence' and attainment, school and external examinations, or in less formal ways, so that pupils may be 'educationally' differentiated and their diverse courses confirmed. (Whether or not teachers — or parents — like this system is another question; they are not solely responsible for its development, nor, in isolation, in a position to change it.) That this is not simply a process of academic assessment has been shown by numerous studies. Douglas's finding that junior school teachers tended to under-estimate the potential of working-class boys when the teachers' assessments were compared to the pupils' scores in 'objective' ability tests is one illustration of this.[1] Rosenthal and Jacobson provide a brief summary of American research on this theme, and focus on one interesting aspect of teachers' assessments — the tendency of them to act as self-fulfilling prophesies, determinants of the pupils' actual attainments.[2]

This leads us to look at the concept of *expectation* again; for although *expectations* cannot be equated with *opinions,* if we exclude all but normative expectations, as Dahrendorf suggests, we introduce another type of artificial restriction. In fact we cannot exclude significant phenomenological processes, such as the way in which 'one person's expectations for another person's behaviour can quite unwittingly become a more accurate prediction, simply for its having been made'.[3] Or, to return to the case of 'Black School', the extent to which the pupils there will 'not allow' teachers to deal leniently with them. By adding this element we have parted company with Dahrendorf, for while he is concerned with an artificial construct, man as role conformer, the attempt here is to examine the ways in which the expectations of different groups act on the incumbents of a particular social position — school teachers — and in interaction with their own expectations, influence their behaviour.

We have emphasized some aspects of what might be called a *structured network of expectations.* Such a concept enables us to interpret the relationships of teachers and pupils in the classroom and to relate this to the differential power positions of different social-class groups in the schools and in the society. The particular structure of a network of relationships is not immutable, it does not imply a massive consensus — though this is not precluded either. The concept of function (or dysfunction) as applied to the degree of agreement or disagreement about expectations is incompatible with this formulation. The alternative, suggested here, to the functionalist/role approach requires a historical examination of the forces involved in an attempt to trace the characteristics and trends inherent in a particular situation. This, as long as the variation due to personal expectations is integrated, provides a dialectical method of exploring the processes of social interaction in schools.

---

[1] J. W. B. Douglas, *The Home and the School* (London, 1964), ch. 9.
[2] R. Rosenthal and L. Jacobson, *Pygmalion in the Classroom* (New York, 1968).
[3] *Ibid.* p. vii.

A REDUNDANT CONCEPT ...

It has been the intention in this paper to demonstrate some of the main inadequacies of role theory and to suggest an alternative approach. The argument has been illustrated with reference to the field of education for two main reasons. Firstly, this area has received a good deal of attention from role theorists and from functionalists generally. Secondly, many students of education and of the sociology of education (perhaps to a greater extent than students of general sociology) are presented with only this sociological orientation and as if it were the only one. The views, that the school is a stage for role performances, or an integrated system for role allocation and role learning, are not the only sociological perspectives available. Sociology as a discipline is characterized by major controversies (even if these are underplayed most of the time), and no student who does not recognize this is in a position to evaluate or criticize the particular brands of sociological formulations which he or she is taught.

The problems of role theory are not, in fact, separable from the problems of sociology itself. Preiss and Ehrlich come nearer than most other writers in recognizing this relationship. They note that many researchers who have used role concepts have found them inadequate.

Nevertheless, these inadequacies have rarely shaken the researchers' faith in their initial assumptions about role behaviour and role theory. The strength of this attachment seems to us to derive from the very pervasiveness of role, and cognate concepts in contemporary sociological and psychological theories. *Given such pervasiveness, the acceptance reformulation or rejection of contemporary role schemas is of prodigious importance.* To reject role theory is to call for a revolution in social science and such scientific revolutions demand the presentation of a new body of research or a new paradigm which cogently reinterprets the existing body of relevant knowledge. To seek *reformulation, as is our objective,* we need to recognize that the problems of role theory are inextricably bound with the general problems of sociology and social psychology.[1]

But one does not have to be committed to the concept of role to recognize that both its appeal and its problems are related to problems in general sociology. And it is either arrogant, or very naive to assert that only one model of explanation is available. In view of the confusions and distortions inseparable from the concept of role, its popularity does not seem to us to be sufficient ground for defending it. If sociology is to be developed as a viable, and humane discipline, we need to be prepared not only to seek new bodies of theory and research, but also to weed out those of the established ones which are redundant; to reject the concept of role would contribute to such a process.

1   J. Preiss and H. Ehrlich, *Examination of Role Theory,* pp. 160-1.

6

ROLE PERFORMANCES AND SOCIAL COMPARISON PROCESSES

JOHN URRY

INTRODUCTION

The concepts of both role and reference group have emerged out of the symbolic interactionist tradition. There are two key processes discussed within the latter: the first is the way in which the individual internalizes the attitudes of various others by taking their role; the second is that as a consequence he comes to see himself through the eyes of these various others, he becomes an object of his own consciousness. Some attention has been paid in the literature as to the way in which the reference group concept has helped to elucidate the former process;[1] this article is intended to indicate how satisfactory explanation of the latter process demands consideration not only of role theory but also of certain alternative aspects of reference group analysis.

The term reference group was first used by Hyman in 1942;[2] in this long article he distinguished between the identificatory and judgmental orientations that an actor could take to an object of reference. This distinction was made explicit by Kelly in 1952 when he distinguished between the normative and comparative functions of a reference group.[3] Further conceptual elaboration has resulted in the popular analytical distinction between a normative and a comparative reference group. This distinction corresponds to the processes discussed within symbolic interactionism. The focus of interest in this article is not upon showing the relationship between the norms and values of an actor's objects of normative reference (which may vary in degree of salience),[4] but upon the way in which an actor stands back from himself and evaluates his performance within a particular role in comparison with various others.

1   See for example, Maureen E. Cain, 'Some suggested developments for role and reference group analysis', *The British Journal of Sociology*, 19 (1968), 191-205, and R. Dahrendorf, 'Homo sociologicus', in *Essays in the Theory of Society* (London, 1968), pp. 19-87, especially pp. 44-52.
2   H. H. Hyman, 'The psychology of status', *Archives of Psychology*, no. 269 (1942).
3   See H. H. Kelly, 'Two functions of reference groups', in H. H. Hyman and Eleanor Singer (eds.), *Readings in Reference Group Theory and Research* (New York, 1968), pp. 77-83.
4   See, for example, Cain, 'Some suggested developments' and R. H. Turner, 'Role-taking, role standpoint, and reference-group behaviour', in B. J. Biddle and E. J. Thomas (eds.), *Role Theory: Concepts and Research* (New York, 1966), pp. 151-9.

A comparative reference group may be defined as any social object with which an actor compares himself and which consequently acts as a basis of self-evaluation. This notion is based upon the anthropological necessity that where there is a need for self-evaluation and where there are no direct physical standards by which an actor can judge himself he will rely on certain social bases of judgement. It is somewhat surprising that although this has been a clear theme in moral philosophy, contemporary sociology has relatively neglected such considerations.[1] Latane, a dozen years after the first statement of Festinger's theory of social comparisons, says that there has been practically no testing of its key assumptions, while Hyman and Singer talk of the state of neglect into which the comparative reference group concept has fallen.[2] Nevertheless to the extent that an attempt has been made to account for an actor's evaluation of his own role-performances in comparative terms it is quite clear that this attempt has been extraordinarily unsuccessful. It will emerge later why this is so; for the present it is necessary to consider the most significant contribution that has been produced in this field. Much of the rest of this article is a discussion of certain themes raised but not always answered by W. G. Runciman's *Relative Deprivation and Social Justice.*[3]

W. G. RUNCIMAN

This work is important for three reasons: the multidimensionality of study; the concentration upon inequalities within the wider society; and the attempt to derive normative prognostications. It is a little dubious whether the book lives up to these admirable organizing principles. Firstly, consideration will be paid to the brief but idiosyncratic explanation of the promotion finding in the American Soldier; secondly, attention will be focussed upon Runciman's interpretation of modern social history; finally, some criticism will be made of the methodology of his sample survey. The depth of interest in this particular work is, it must be noted, a reflection of its importance.

AMERICAN SOLDIERS

The *American Soldier* promotion finding is that in response to the question: Do you think a soldier with ability has a good chance for promotion in the army? the pattern of responses was that

Air Corps men tended to take a dimmer view of promotion opportunities for men of ability . . . than did the Military Police . . . [although] chances of promotion . . .

---

1 See H. Schoeck, *Envy* (London, 1969) for a discussion of this.
2 B. Latane, 'Studies in social comparison – introduction and over-view', *Journal of Experimental Social Psychology,* Supplement 1, *Studies in Social Comparison* (September 1960), pp. 1-5, especially p. 1; H. H. Hyman and Eleanor Singer, 'Introduction' in Hyman and Singer, *Reference Group Theory,* pp. 1-21, especially p. 18.
3 See W. G. Runciman, *Relative Deprivation and Social Justice. A Study of Attitudes to Social Inequality in Twentieth Century England* (London, 1966).

were about the worst in any branch of the Army — among this sample of men in the Army one to two years, only 24 per cent of MP's were noncoms as compared with 47 per cent of the Air Corps men.[1]

This was, it should be noted, a general relationship found throughout the American army, and one that could not be explained in terms of cultural differences between high and low promotion-rate units.[2] The Research Board's explanation is simply that: 'such opinions . . . [with respect to promotion] represent a relationship between their expectations and their achievements relative to others *in the same boat with them*';[3] Merton argues that a 'high rate of mobility induces excessive hopes and expectations among members of the group so that each is more likely to experience a sense of frustration in his present position and disaffection with the chances of promotion';[4] and Runciman, who claims to be generalizing Merton, claims that

Those who were not promoted in the Military Police tended to compare themselves with the large number of their fellows who were also not promoted, while those few who had been promoted were likely to appear to themselves to have done relatively better. In the Air Corps, by contrast, the man who was not promoted would be likely to compare himself with the large number of his fellows who *had* been promoted, while these, though successful, would appear to themselves to have done relatively less well.[5]

Runciman thus maintains that the promoted always compare themselves with the promoted, while the non-promoted compare themselves with the other non-promoted where few are promoted but with the promoted if many are promoted.[6] This seems improbable. On the one hand, with respect to the promoted one might expect that either they would compare themselves with the non-promoted, or if not then because of the general character of the evaluation implied in the question the greater the promotion rate the *greater* the satisfaction that would result. On the other hand, Runciman's 'numerical' explanation[7] of the sentiments of the non-promoted implies a sharp cut-off point at which there is a sudden shift of the comparison to the promoted; Brian Barry argues both that there is no evidence for it and that it contradicts Runciman's curvilinear relationship outlined just after.[8]

1 S. A. Stouffer *et al., The American Soldier* (New York, 1949), vol. 1, p. 251.
2 On the generality of this relationship see *ibid.* pp. 254-8; the inapplicability of a cultural explanation arises because of the fact that morale was generally highest in the Air Corps, see *ibid.* p. 253 and ch. 7.
3 *Ibid.* p. 251.
4 R. K. Merton and Alice S. Rossi, 'Contributions to the theory of reference group behaviour', in R. K. Merton, *Social Theory and Social Structure* (New York, 1957), pp. 225-80, especially p. 237.
5 Runciman, *Relative Deprivation*, p. 18.
6 See B. Barry, 'On the roots of social injustice', *Oxford Review*, no. 3 (Michaelmas 1966), 38.
7 Runciman, *Relative Deprivation*, p. 19.
8 See Barry, 'Social injustice', p. 39; on the curvilinear relationship see Merton and Rossi, 'Reference group behaviour', p. 236 and *ibid.* p. 20.

The reason for Runciman's actors being pressganged into making their somewhat bizarre comparisons is that he has to explain the entire process of an actor experiencing relative deprivation, or satisfaction, with respect to a particular reward by the single concept of the comparative reference group. The problems implied by this can be seen from considering his conceptualization of relative deprivation; thus an actor is relatively deprived of X when he does not have X, he sees some other person having X, he wants X, and sees it feasible that he should have X.[1] Now although one may wish to criticize this particular formulation it is important in pointing out that there are a number of separate analytical stages by which a situation of inequality is transformed into a sentiment of relative deprivation. Nevertheless in Runciman's account the single variable of the comparative reference group is used to explain all of these stages; thus a necessary and sufficient condition for relative deprivation for Runciman is that an actor compares himself with a particular social object with respect to a particular reward of which he has less.

Four further points need making. First of all, the reconsideration of Runciman's specification of the process through which relative deprivation is derived suggests at least three stages: the perception of inequality, the comparison with the particular social object, and the evaluation of this as unjust and the outcome of potentially changeable conditions. The second point is that the relationship between these stages is only contingent and not necessary; thus the fact that an actor compares his inferior reward of X with that of one or more others does not mean that he will necessarily interpret the rewards accruing to his performance within that role as unjust. To argue that is to argue that all social systems are necessarily illegitimate; it is to ignore the specific mechanisms found in practically all societies which serve to justify the patterns of inequality found within them. Thirdly, it is noteworthy that Runciman's explanation in terms of this single variable results in its reification. While phenomenologically an actor's comparisons are intermittent, inconsistent and segmental, within his analysis they are conceptually reified into his notion of the actor's precise, unambiguous and unchangeable comparative reference group. Reification of this sort results in a failure to consider the many comparisons an actor may make, the variable nature of the object with which he compares himself, the different meanings of 'in-' as opposed to 'out-groups' comparisons, and the failure to distinguish between an actor's object of comparison and the audience within which one's role-performances are judged. And finally it should be noted that there have been two further systematic attempts to explain this promotion finding; these cannot be discussed in detail here but it is interesting that Brian Barry's is a numerical explanation, while conceptual reification abounds in that of James Davis.[2]

---

1   *Ibid.* p. 10.
2   See Barry, 'Social injustice', and J. Davis, 'A formal interpretation of the theory of relative deprivation', *Sociometry,* 22 (1959), 280-96.

MEN IN HISTORY

In the remainder of his work Runciman makes some use of the generalization that the higher the actor's social ranking the more, rather than the less, relative deprivation that results. Specifically he argues that manual workers have extremely restricted comparative reference groups; indeed, although their relative deprivation with respect to status is increasing, their class deprivation is argued to be on the wane. Certain non-manual workers make wider and more class-conscious comparisons. Before discussing the survey from which this conclusion is derived it is necessary to consider his account of recent British social history.

This is so not simply because of its undoubted intrinsic interest but also because of Runciman's explicit methodological pronouncement that by itself the sample survey is no more than a snap-shot of social reality at one time and place, and thus that it is only the historical account which can provide an explanation of the findings revealed in the sample survey. The latter he claims is merely descriptive; it is only the historical survey which is explanatory.[1] The evaluation therefore of *Relative Deprivation and Social Justice* as a contribution to sociological theory rests upon the utility of the historical explanation.

The first point to note is that this explanation rests very heavily upon changes within the standard of living; thus he says that 'there are some points between which satisfaction rises as equality spreads, but others between which an improving situation leads to a higher, not lower, incidence of relative deprivation'.[2] The problem with this sort of explanation, that is in terms of enhanced and frustrated aspirations, is that it renders unnecessary the notion of a comparative reference group. An example of this can be seen from where Runciman quotes Henry Pelling to the effect that the onset of the great depression 'actually discouraged working class militancy and destroyed the "advanced" elements then in existence'.[3] Runciman's interpretation of this is that 'such a tendency can perhaps be explained by the cautious pessimism which hardship inevitably breeds. But this, in effect, is to say that in hard times comparative reference groups will be more restricted than in good, which is part of the generalisation being put forward'.[4]

The point is that the insertion of the term 'comparative reference group' is quite unnecessary since it neither explains the 'cautious pessimism' nor provides an alternative account of this lack of dissent in terms other than the response to this particular hardship. A later example shows explicitly that the comparisons made by an actor are quite redundant to Runciman's explanation of dissent. When discussing the new scales of relief under the Unemployment Act of 1934, he says that 'the frustration of modest expectations led . . . to a more intense and widespread sense of relative deprivation';[5] thus there is posited a more or less

1 See Runciman, *Relative Deprivation*, pp. 6-7 and 217.
2 *Ibid.* p. 21.
3 H. Pelling, *The Origins of the Labour Party, 1880-1900* (London, 1953), p. 6.
4 Runciman, *Relative Deprivation*, p. 21.
5 *Ibid.* p. 67.

necessary relationship between expectations frustrated and relative deprivation, and the derivation of self-evaluatory attitudes in comparison with others is quite unnecessary. Furthermore the only way by which Runciman knows of the existence of relative deprivation is because of the actual expression of dissent. Thus the argument is that frustrated expectations lead to dissent, the notions of the comparative reference group and relative deprivation being quite unnecessary to the account. This can be seen from Runciman's observations that follow, commencing with the situation at the end of the first world war:

The sense of relative deprivation among the working class was unmistakeably high, not only in terms of class, but of status and power. The story of the period between the two wars, therefore, is a decline or, at least, a considerable appeasement, of relative deprivation among the less fortunately placed . . . The Depression served to pare down reference groups as effectively as the war served to heighten them . . . The Depression reduced rather than heightened the magnitude and intensity of relative deprivation because few of its victims felt it to be obviously avoidable.[1]

But firstly, how is it known that at the end of the first world war the sense of relative deprivation among the working class was noticeably high except in terms of the actual expression of dissent; secondly, how can it be argued that there was a long-run decline in relative deprivation again in terms other than the fact of dissent, and more especially, is relative deprivation something that just remains being quietly appeased or is it something that is both focussed and requires continual reinvigoration; and thirdly, how is a reconciliation reached between maintaining that the lack of dissent in the depression was the result of the paring-down of comparative reference groups and that it acted through the permeation of a sense of unavoidability? In general Runciman fails to consider what it is to be an actor within an environing structure. Thus, firstly, the response to a rising standard of living is not simply an expansion of the range of comparative reference groups *pari passu,* since between such changes and the selection of comparative reference groups lies an actor's structure of meaning; and secondly, various changes may occur within the structure of society which will differentially affect the process by which 'rising optimism' is transformed into relative deprivation.

Thus the intermittent insertion of the terms 'comparative reference group' and 'relative deprivation' in no way renders Runciman's account of this history sociological. This is not incidentally to claim that it is historically invalid, or without sociological interest, but that it does not provide a systematic sociological explanation of the selection and consequences of comparative reference group processes. The sample survey is located within a historical vacuum.

1   *Ibid.* pp. 59-60.

MEN IN A SURVEY

Strangely, however, Runciman commences by introducing two variables, high/medium/low income and self-rated class, which he suggests are independent and might be explanatory. However, not only does this contradict the methodological pronouncement above, but the income variable suffers from the disadvantages already mentioned with respect to the standard of living, while there are four objections to Runciman's claim that

If nine-tenths of English adults see themselves as belonging to one or other of two separate social categories [middle/working-class], and if these categories carry strong overtones not only of job or income but a style of life, values and outlook, then it is plausible to interpret their self-assigned 'class' as implying a choice of a normative reference group.[1]

Firstly, the questions asked in the survey forced the respondent to give only a middle- or working-class response;[2] secondly, Runciman himself admits the enormous variation in the meaning which actors accord to these particular social categories;[3] thirdly, there is no evidence that a forced statement of self-rated class gives any indication that the chosen category will actually be of any normative significance; and finally, Runciman makes the following point that

It may be very misleading to speak of attitudes relevant to social inequality being 'caused' by the choice of normative reference group. This choice may itself be determined by other influences which are themselves the cause of attitudes to inequality, so that self-rating would be better described as a symptom of these attitudes than a determinant of them.[4]

He continues by suggesting a possible determinant:

It is known that self-assessment varies with the occupational composition of the immediate neighbourhood in which people live; but in a national poll-type sample such comparisons are not feasible.[5]

What may be significant is that this immediate neighbourhood is a determinant not only of self-rating but also of the patterning of comparative reference group choices; but regrettably Runciman's methodology prevents this from being considered. All the survey permits is a description of the patterning of such choices; how effective is this description?

Attention will be firstly devoted to his treatment of class.[6] In his theoretical

1   *Ibid.* p. 164.
2   This can be seen from questions 20(a) and (b). The former is: 'What social class would you say you belonged to?' Respondents answering other, don't know, none, etc., are asked: 'If you *had* to say middle or working class, which would you say?'
3   See tables 2, 3 and 4, pp. 158-62, *ibid.*
4   *Ibid.* pp. 164-5.
5   *Ibid.* p. 165.
6   Runciman distinguishes between three dimensions of social inequality, class, status and party; see *ibid.* ch. 3. Runciman does not however consider the comparative references operative within the power dimension.

discussion he maintains that an actor's class situation includes not only income differences, but also differences in opportunities for upward mobility, advantages in kind, provision for retirement, security of employment and the work-situation *à la* Lockwood.[1] Nevertheless, his operational definition of this is that of wealth, since he only considers the dimensions of income, consumer-goods and state welfare provision. The objection here is not to the consideration of such economic inequalities and the felt deprivations, but to the suggestion that these give any necessary indication of the nature of class relationships within society. But even if this is so, they still raise methodological problems of some significance. The key section is clearly that on incomes, and the key question is 9 (a).[2] Two objections can be made to the latter: firstly, it asks about other 'sorts' of people and thus indicates to the respondents that what is required is a specification neither of single individuals nor of other groups or collectivities, but essentially of other social categories;[3] and secondly, by asking whether 'at the moment' such a comparison is being articulated, attention is directed toward recent changes in the economic hierarchy and away from more long-run developments. Similar criticisms can be directed against the succeeding questions, 10 (a) and (b);[4] firstly, the use of the term 'nowadays' is suggestive of an insignificant time-span, and secondly, the very terms 'manual workers' and 'white-collar workers', obtained from empirical sociology rather than from the phenomenological experience of actors within a class structure, are hardly likely to evoke sentiments of intense class deprivation.

Runciman's argument with respect to status is similarly problematic. He notes initially that it is not usefully possible to ask respondents how much status they have, they ought to have, and how much other people have. Nevertheless, this chapter is intended to provide evidence for the view that relative deprivation of status among the less fortunate has been increasing with the advance towards some greater measure of equality. But this is difficult to show not only because of the descriptive quality of the sample survey but because of the indirect nature of the information available. Thus some reliance is placed upon the respondents' attitudes to the education and careers of their children. Yet as Runciman himself points out many people will express higher aspirations for their children than they would for themselves. Consequently, the fact that 82 per cent of manual workers would like their son to have a university education is like saying that most parents would prefer

1   Thus he says: 'to speak of a person's "class" is to speak of his approximate, shared location in the economic hierarchy'; this is *ibid.* p. 38. Also see D. Lockwood, *The Blackcoated Worker* (London, 1958).
2   This question is: 'Do you think there are any other sorts of people doing noticeably better at the moment than you and your family?'
3   See R. K. Merton, 'Continuities in the theory of reference groups and social structure', in Merton, *Social Theory*, pp. 281-386, especially pp. 285-6, and 299-300.
4   These are: 'Some people say that manual workers are doing much better nowadays than white-collar workers. Do you think that this is so or not?' 'Do you think that manual workers ought to be doing as well as they are doing compared with white-collar workers?'

their children to have well- rather than badly-paid jobs.[1] A good example of a pair
of non-educational questions designed to show the same is provided by 14 (a) and
(b).[2] But since only 17 per cent of all respondents wanted to leave where they lived
for reasons connected with the district, since that motive for leaving is not
necessarily indicative of status aspiration, and since 14 (b) is a clearly leading
question, there is little to support the claim that there is a high degree of status
aspiration.

It is now necessary to consider certain substantive and methodological issues
raised by Runciman's provocative study.

MATTERS OF SUBSTANCE

The first point, that is not discussed at all, relates to the argument above that
the making of a comparison does not necessarily entail a sentiment of relative
deprivation. It was there pointed out that this occurs because an actor, although
he compares himself with a more fortunate other, considers the inequality
legitimate. What was not there shown was one well-documented reason for this,
namely, that the actor's interpretation of his position along one dimension does
not take place in a cognitive vacuum; thus, his evaluation of whether it is justifiable
that he is deprived along one dimension depends upon his ranking along other
dimensions which are in some sense relevant to it. Martin Patchen thus suggests
that in the specific context of wage bargaining the actor undergoes a cognitive
interpretation of the sort, my pay: his pay, compared to my position on dimensions
related to pay (skill, seniority, education and so on): his position on such
dimensions.[3] At the same time however this is not to argue that the theory of
status congruence is a better explanation of the outcomes of, say, political
radicalism or racial prejudice.[4] Most research in that field is inadequate, firstly,
because of the neglect of time and thus of the development, salience, and effects
of a situation of status incongruence, and secondly, because no attention is paid
to the specific audience object in terms of which the actor engages in certain role-
performances in particular ways. In other words, the typical actor is not interested
in the acquisition of status (or even of power or economic rewards) in society as a
whole but rather in relation to a specific audience or audiences. There is thus the
possibility of compensatory statuses, of concealing certain statuses through

1   See Runciman, *Relative Deprivation*, pp. 228-31.
2   These are: 'Would you like to move out of your present district? Is this anything to do with
    the sort of district (you think) it is?'
3   See M. Patchen, *The Choice of Wage Comparisons* (New Jersey, 1961), and 'A conceptual
    framework and some empirical data regarding comparisons of social rewards', in Hyman and
    Singer, *Reference Group Theory*, pp. 166-84.
4   See Runciman's discussion of both these phenomena: W. G. Runciman, 'Justice, congruence
    and Professor Homans', *European Journal of Sociology*, 8 (1967), 115-28; and W. G.
    Runciman and C. Bagley, 'Relative deprivation, status consistency, and attitudes to
    immigrants', *Sociology*, 3 (1969), 359-75.

audience segregation and playing-at-a-role, of deviant ranking within particular dimensions, of alternative dimensions such as beauty or eroticism, and of the irrelevance of some dimensions within certain social contexts.

There have been two main attempts to integrate these considerations relating to the theory of status congruence with the study of social comparison processes. Johan Galtung distinguishes between a TU position ('topdog' – 'underdog' along different dimensions) and a UU position ('underdog' along both dimensions) and maintains that aggression is more probable in the former.[1] This follows, firstly, because the latter has less resources for aggression and less potential for developing self-righteous claims for equality with TT ('topdog' along both dimensions), secondly, because the disequilibriated is never left in peace with his disequilibrium unless he cuts out certain interaction channels, and thirdly, because the TU will use TT as his reference group even if he is a member of UU. The TU thus has relative deprivation built into his situation. The other contribution here is that of Anderson and Zelditch who make two points ignored by Galtung.[2] Firstly, they point out that no effects are going to result from a situation of status incongruence unless some actual comparison process does occur. The second point is to emphasize that the patterning of relative deprivation does not necessarily follow from the overall structure; thus, even if an actor compares himself with another, he may say, either, 'I'm doing quite well since I make as much money as B although he has more prestige', or 'Although I make as much money as B, he still does not accept me'.[3] Furthermore, even in the second case, relative deprivation and dissent need not follow, since the actor's attempt to change his situation may be mitigated either by insulation, that is, in-group interaction and comparison, or by mobility.[4]

A second area of substantive research is indicated in Runciman's specification of relative deprivation where he points out that the actor must see it as feasible that he should acquire the good in question, that is, the actor must feel in some sense or other that he is justified in making the comparison. Form and Geschwender maintain that an actor cannot evaluate his own occupational position by comparing himself with others unless such others are in an occupation in some sense comparable to his own.[5] What this leaves, though, as problematic is the nature of the comparability. Helen Strauss' study of social comparison processes among the blind is interesting in showing, firstly, that one-fifth of her respondents did not compare themselves with anyone (in terms of the dimensions being studied), secondly, the great majority of comparisons were with the non-blind in their

1   See J. Galtung, 'A structural theory of aggression', *Journal of Peace Research*, 2 (1964), 95-119.
2   See B. Anderson and M. Zelditch, 'Rank equilibrium and political behaviour', *European Journal of Sociology*, 5 (1964), 112-24.
3   See *ibid.* p. 115.
4   See *ibid.* p. 118.
5   See W. H. Form and J. A. Geschwender, 'Social reference basis of job satisfaction: the case of manual workers', in Hyman and Singer, *Reference Group Theory*, pp. 185-98.

immediate social environment, and thirdly, since their inferiority cannot be laid at the door of their own self such comparisons were not psychologically disturbing.[1] The second point, the argument that propinquity is the basis, or at least an extremely important basis, for the selection of comparative references was a key point in the original article written by Hyman in 1942 when he said,

The rare occurence of the total population as a reference group and the great frequency of more intimate reference groups are characteristic of the process of judging status. Individuals operate for the most part in small groups within the total society, and the total population may have little relevance for them. Far more important are their friends, people they work with.[2]

Thus Form and Geschwender maintain that manual workers evaluate their occupational success by comparing themselves with the peers with whom they began life;[3] Reissman explains the low aspiration of policemen in terms of their high rate of mobility in relation to their brothers;[4] while Stern and Keller's analysis in France reveals a low degree of class resentment, a high emphasis upon family and friends as comparison objects, and a low propensity to cite non-membership groups at all.[5] Stern and Keller make two other points. First of all, they find that it is mainly 'the upper-class people' who tend to explain the differences of social class in terms of the 'system'; 'lower-class people' are more prone to blame personalities.[6] They explain this by arguing that it follows from the fact that the survey was conducted in France rather than say higher-mobility USA where one would expect self-interpretation among the successful and system-interpretation among the unsuccessful. This is perhaps dubious since it ignores the many constraints placed upon systemic interpretations by the underprivileged. The second point they make is that the aim of such comparisons is essentially to arrive at the harmonious continuance of social relationships with one's friends, neighbours and workmates.[7]

Two briefer substantive points need also to be made. Firstly, Runciman's stratification perspective precludes consideration of the interrelationships between the different dimensions of power, status, and economic rewards, and especially of how inequalities and felt deprivations within one may help to determine those in the other dimensions.[8] A second point is that although there is much plausibility in

1   See Helen Strauss, 'Reference group and social comparison processes among the totally blind', *ibid.* pp. 222-37.
2   Hyman, 'Psychology of status', p. 24; on the following page he points out the importance of reference individuals as opposed to reference groups.
3   See Form and Geschwender, 'Social reference basis', p. 197.
4   See L. Reissman, 'Levels of aspiration and social class', *American Sociological Review,* 18 (1953), 233-42.
5   See E. Stern and Suzanne Keller, 'Spontaneous group references in France', in Hyman and Singer, *Reference Group Theory,* pp. 199-206.
6   *Ibid.* p. 205.
7   See *ibid.* p. 206.
8   For a similar criticism of Runciman's approach see G. K. Ingham, 'Social stratification: individual attributes and social relationships', *Sociology,* 4 (1970), 105-13.

all the literature above which emphasizes the propinquitous nature of the comparer and the comparison object, the following point made by Runciman seems extremely important. He says that 'reference groups tend to be closely circumscribed at all levels of society except under some abnormal stimulus';[1] this has immense implications for the methodology of social comparisons research.

MATTERS OF METHODOLOGY

The reason for the importance of this point is that it will be remembered that Runciman's historical account, although interesting, did not provide an explanation of the descriptive evidence revealed by the sample survey. The latter is thus placed within a historical vacuum; in consequence there are no good grounds for extrapolating his findings to another time or place; or for believing that the attitudes there revealed have any relationship to the actions of actors located within history. In 1962 at the time of the survey was there an 'abnormal stimulus', if so, how important was it, and what effect did it have, or if not, what patterning of comparisons would have resulted if there had been such a stimulus? Thus what can be concluded from the fact that this sample had restricted comparisons in 1962 as to their actual actions within the world in 1962, or their attitudes in any other temporal or spatial location? The singularly individualistic presuppositions of the interview situation prevent this from being considered. That such comparisons occur within history, relate to each other historically, and themselves have a history, are all typically ignored. The social scientific attempt to systematize these historical processes as suggested within both moral philosophy and Marxian writings on class consciousness results as in Runciman in a-historical, reified configurations of comparative reference group selection that bear no obvious relationship to men's actions within the world.

There is however an even more profound methodological point which is relevant here; this derives from the consideration not of the relationship of these attitudes to men's actions or to men in different spatial and temporal locations, but rather from whether in *that* time and place these attitudes revealed are in fact accurate representations of the attitudes held.

There are two possibilities; the first is most devastating. Merton and Rossi point out that there is no reason to presume that comparisons with others are uniformly conscious and thus there may be all sorts of unwitting responses that an actor may make.[2] Thus if an actor provides no external references it is unclear whether this is because he does not make such comparisons or simply that the questions asked failed to elicit them. Further, once one has found out the comparisons made by an actor one simply does not know whether they are salient for him. Merton and Rossi maintain that non-sample survey techniques are implied; perhaps Anderson and

1   Runciman, *Relative Deprivation*, p. 195.
2   See Merton and Rossi, 'Reference group behaviour', p. 249.

Zelditch are right in arguing, 'A discriminating "clinical" interview searching for the "meanings" which the rank dimensions and symbols attached to these have for different upwardly and downwardly mobile persons might conceivably enable us to infer something about the interplay of the processes we have discussed, but the standard survey procedure is clearly inadequate'.[1]

That is, in itself, a profound criticism of Runciman's procedure; yet, even if one supposes that all comparisons are in fact conscious it is quite clear that the actual patterning revealed by any particular set of questions significantly relates to the structure of questions asked. This has already been mentioned above in discussing Runciman; the importance of the point was, however, difficult to evaluate. It can perhaps be better shown by considering the questions asked in two of the more interesting studies already mentioned. Thus Helen Strauss derives her findings from a battery of three questions which preclude the sighted being ignored as an object with which the blind could compare themselves with respect to appearance, learning and character.[2] The main question asked by Stern and Keller, on the other hand, is very different for two reasons.[3] Firstly, by referring to 'the standard of living of the French people' attention is directed away from groups or collectivities in structured conflict with each other; it is rather something which may rise or fall for everyone. Secondly, no indication is given to the respondents that the question should be answered in terms of anything other than a personal, non-relational framework.

CONCLUSION

So far nothing has been said of the final section of Runciman's work in which he advocates a political philosophy (Rawls's contract model of social justice) based upon an egoistic psychology in which multiple interest groups reach a dubious equilibrium through the resolution of their contradictory claims, by reference to an increasingly articulate conception of social justice.[4] Reference group analysis is an ideal accompaniment of this since through reification it makes somewhat more definite and explicit the nature of this equilibrium. The argument here, on the other hand, emphasizes the incorrectness of the egoistic psychological model, maintains that justice is more than a reciprocity of fair treatment, and that the study of social comparisons must develop in ways not found in Runciman's work. The discussion of the substantive and methodological issues in this article is an attempt to provide the basis for such development.

1   See *ibid.* pp. 249-50; Anderson and Zelditch, 'Rank equilibrium', p. 124.
2   These took the form: 'In judging your own personal appearance, are you likely to think of yourself in comparison with (men/women) of your own age who are blind, or who are sighted?'
3   This is: 'We are making a study of the standard of living of the French people, but we realise that when one speaks of the standard of living, everyone understands something different by that expression. I would therefore like to ask you what would be, for you, a satisfactory standard of living?'
4   See T. Burns, 'Review of Runciman', *British Journal of Sociology*, 17 (1966), 430-4.

7

REPLY TO MR URRY

W. G. RUNCIMAN

The Editor has invited me to reply to Mr Urry's paper, and I am grateful both to him for giving me the opportunity of doing so and to Mr Urry for the attention which he has devoted to my book. Since, as it happens, I have very recently dealt elsewhere with a number of the issues which Urry raises,[1] I think the best thing for me to do here is simply to take Urry's criticisms in the order in which he advances them and make a few short comments on each.

1. I readily agree not only that (as I made clear in the book) there are several possible explanations of the well-known *American Soldier* finding but also that (as I failed to make sufficiently clear) to say that it is most readily explicable by reference to the comparisons which the soldiers sampled may be supposed to have made is only to say that this is the most immediately plausible way of explaining it away. The point which I was concerned to make was that the lack of a correlation between objective inequality and resentment of it is not so paradoxical as may at first appear. In this case, the air of paradox is dispelled as soon as we remember the truism that one's sense of grievance, or lack of it, is very much a matter of what comparison one draws. For what it is worth, I still think it likely that the responses of men in the Military Police who were not promoted were connected with the fact that there was a sufficient possibility of promotion for them not to feel hopelessly disadvantaged but not so much that they would come to feel as well entitled to it as their numerous former equals who *had* been promoted. But the full answer, if we could ever discover it, would undoubtedly be more complicated than that.

It likewise goes without saying that an S-shaped relation between inequality and grievance is not going to apply universally over the whole range of social inequalities of different kinds. But again, my point was only that there are a lot of contexts where it can as plausibly be expected as a linear relation. It was for this reason that I cited an example deliberately taken from a quite different area of sociological research from the study of inequalities of opportunity within a specifically military context — the so-called 'disaster studies' analysed by Allan H. Barton[2] — and

---

1 In a lecture entitled '*Relative Deprivation and Social Justice:* Some Lessons of Hindsight' given at the University of Sussex in March 1971, to be reprinted in C. R. Bagley (ed.), *Concepts and Methods of Social Research,* and as a Postscript to the forthcoming Pelican edition of the book.

2 Allan H. Barton, *Social Organization under Stress: a Sociological Review of Disaster Studies* (Washington D.C., 1963), cited in *Relative Deprivation and Social Justice,* p. 23, n. 21.

suggested a number of other historical contexts where it might also be found. In any given case, it is then a matter of empirical research to see whether an S-shaped relation does hold and if so whether there is any evidence to indicate who was in fact comparing themselves with who.

2. I do not 'have to explain the entire process of an actor experiencing relative deprivation . . . by the single concept of the comparative reference group' and I would be foolish to try; the explanation, if it can be found, depends on identifying the influences which caused a particular comparison to be made and therewith a sense of relative deprivation engendered. Nor is it for me a 'sufficient condition for relative deprivation that an actor compares himself with a particular social object with respect to a particular reward of which he has less'; as Urry himself points out a few lines earlier, the actor has also to want that reward and see it as feasible that he should have it. Nor can 'the process through which relative deprivation is derived' consist in three stages of which the first two are 'the perception of inequality' and 'the comparison with the particular social object'; the first of these already logically implies the presence of the second. On the other hand when Urry goes on to say, as though consequentially, that a person can compare his reward with the higher reward of someone else without necessarily thinking his own reward unjust, I agree entirely. Indeed I am at a loss to see on what grounds anyone could hold otherwise.

The more serious point which Urry touches on in this section of his paper is that to identify a particular comparison as decisive, or even as 'salient', is to impose an artificial rigidity on the fluid and ambiguous comparisons which people actually make. But the answer to this is that although it is perfectly true that people's actual choices of reference groups (which aren't really *choices* at all) are admittedly fluid and ambiguous it is a matter of fact also that a particular comparison *can* sometimes be identified as decisive in a particular context. This is one of the conclusions which emerges from the experimental literature on social comparison, whatever may be its other inadequacies, and I cited some of it for this very reason.

3. When I said that only historical evidence could really explain the findings of my sample survey, I did not mean either that a survey can never be so designed as to test one or more specifically causal hypotheses or that a survey may not, although purely descriptive itself, furnish a test of a causal hypothesis derived from evidence of another kind. What counts as explanation as against a description is always a matter of the context in which it is asked for. All that I meant was that for purposes such as mine a sample survey was bound to be inadequate on its own, since it couldn't tell me what were the historical and cultural influences which might account for the pattern of responses which the survey had disclosed. As it is, I still can't pretend to have furnished the explanation. I can only claim that I have furnished evidence to suggest some possible influences which might account for the social comparisons made, or not made, by my respondents. Unfortunately, it isn't possible to blend the two into a single narrative in the absence of thorough-going biographical research. But I am puzzled by Urry's objection to what I said, since I

made this point precisely because I *agree* with what he says about the inadequacy of the concept of reference groups by itself to explain my findings and the importance which he later assigns to the 'various changes which may occur within the structure of society'.

4. In the same way, I agree that 'comparisons made by an actor are quite redundant' to the explanation of dissent, if by this is meant that the comparison is not the *cause*. Of course it isn't. The cause we are looking for is an antecedent, independent variable of some kind which will account for the salience of the comparison in fact made when other comparisons lay equally well to hand. To cite the salient comparison is, however, to add *something* to a phrase like 'cautious pessimism', since this, however well it describes the state of mind of those concerned, is so unspecific as not to furnish even a hint as to the way in which their expectations have come to be pared down to this degree. When Urry then says that I don't know that people are actually feeling relatively deprived except 'because of the actual expression of dissent', my reaction is again to say: but of course. How else could I expect to know it? By intuition? Whether it is then being appeased, invigorated or what you will is a matter for empirical investigation, and a useful way to start such investigation is, in my view, to look and see who the people in question are comparing themselves with and whether there is reason to think that their comparisons are likely to be shifted in one direction or another as a result of some identifiable external change.

5. I do not understand what Urry means when he says that my account is not 'sociological'. But nor do I see that it matters. The term when used in this sort of context by people who describe themselves as sociologists usually means no more than that they approve of the sorts of research which they do themselves and disapprove of the sorts which they don't. My only concern, however, is whether or not I have found the correct answers to the questions which interest me, and I shall be only too pleased if someone else who shares my interest in these questions does better than I have done, whatever professional label he chooses to wear.

6. I fail to see the force of Urry's criticism of my treatment of self-assigned class. So far from 'admitting' the variation in the meaning which it can carry to different respondents, this was one of the things which I set out to discover, and did. But the real interest of my findings, it seems to me, is that once respondents *have* been asked what they mean by assigning themselves to one class rather than another and their self-assignment has been checked in the light of references to 'class' elsewhere in the interview, it turns out that at most only 10 per cent of the answers given are so uncertain or contradictory that no significance can properly be attached to them. The further suggestion that the majority of the self-assignments which *are* meaningful can be interpreted as a normative reference group does not rest, as Urry suggests, simply on the self-assignments themselves but on the consistent correlations which they display with other social and political attitudes. It is of

course possible that these correlations can be explained away in some other terms than mine. But the onus is on Urry to do so.

As to the 'causal' significance of normative reference groups, I ought perhaps to have put more strongly than I did the point that it 'may be very misleading' to speak in these terms: it certainly *is* misleading. On the other hand, I don't want to go so far as to say, as do for example the authors of the *Affluent Worker* study, that 'although workers who claim "middle-class" status may be less likely than others to vote Labour, this tells one nothing at all about the causal processes which are involved'.[1] What it does is help to show where causes might profitably be looked for, just as does the identification of comparative reference groups in the sort of contexts Urry discusses earlier. Accordingly, I agree with Urry that it is a pity that neighbourhood composition, which I suggested as one possible cause, could not be properly studied in a survey such as mine, and I'm now sorry that I didn't try to include at least something about this in the schedule, however far short it would still have fallen of furnishing the information which only a detailed community study can yield.

7. When it comes to the questions about economic class, I have of course to agree that they did not cover the whole of 'class-situation' and that the attitude questions chosen were bound to yield answers different from those that would have been given if some other wording has been used. What is more, I did not even attempt to measure the *intensity* with which relative deprivation was felt by those who voiced it, although Urry seems to imply that I ought to have. All I was able to attempt was an assessment of the *frequency,* and in one area the *magnitude,* of relative deprivation expressed in response to questions asked of a reasonably representative sample of English people interviewed in their homes. I dare say that if I had used questions deliberately framed to bring out any discernible trace of resentment or envy I would have succeeded in doing so. But this does not, to me, diminish the interest of the responses which I did record. I was myself surprised by these responses precisely because I had tried *not* to phrase the questions in too tendentious a way; but if the conclusions which I drew from them are mistaken, · then let the evidence be produced which shows them to be so. I'm not sure what Urry means when he talks about people's 'phenomenological experience' of class structure, but I suspect he just means their experience; and if he wishes to argue that what people say to an unknown interviewer might be contradicted both by what they would say elsewhere and by what under other circumstances they might actually do, I have no wish to argue with him. All I would say, once again, is that it is up to him to produce the evidence, and whereas I do know of some subsequent research which supports my conclusions[2] I don't yet know of any which invalidates them.

1 John H. Goldthorpe *et al., The Affluent Worker in the Class Structure* (Cambridge, 1969), p. 174.
2 Cf. K. Coates and R. Silburn, *St. Ann's: Poverty, Deprivation and Morale in a Nottingham Community* (Nottingham, 1967), ch. 6 and Dorothy Wedderburn, 'Workplace inequality', *New Society* (9 April 1970), 595.

8. I agree that the evidence provided by the survey on attitudes to status (as distinguished from economic class) is very flimsy. In fact this is, I think, the weakest section of the book. I can again claim that I don't yet know of any evidence that shows my conclusions to be definitely wrong. But the truth is that there just isn't the evidence one way or another to show how far they are plausible. To discover the exact relation between inequalities of status and people's attitudes towards them would be exceedingly difficult even in a community study directed to this purpose,[1] and there is not as far as I know any sociologist who has yet attempted it. The contribution which a sample survey can make to the question is not wholly negligible, but it is certainly bound to be limited.

9. Urry asserts without argument that my 'stratification perspective precludes consideration of the interrelationship between the different dimensions of power, status and economic rewards'. I cannot see why, but since he footnotes an article by G. K. Ingham, whose 'similar criticism' of my approach he endorses, the most useful reply I can make is to refer the reader to my own published rejoinder to Ingham.[2]

10. Urry's concluding remarks about the final section of the book are too fleeting for there to be much purpose in my offering a reply to them. Besides, the proper place for such a controversy would be a journal of philosophy rather than social science. Rawls's conception of justice is not by any means immune to criticism. But its critics need to be armed with more powerful arguments than the simple pronouncement that it is 'based on egoistic psychology' (which, it seems to me, any moral theory must be by definition, unless Urry is a metaphysical holist) or that 'justice is more than a reciprocity of fair treatment' (when the most effective part of Rawls's account of justice is precisely his critique of utilitarianism).

To sum up: I am only too well aware of the deficiencies of my book. But I am doubtful whether Urry's criticisms do much to remedy them. I say this not just because I think Urry's treatment of the notions of 'reference group', 'social comparison' and the rest at least as imprecise as my own, but because the only justification of theoretical or methodological discussion of this kind is its pay-off in empirical research. Urry evidently shares my concern with the question why it is that in twentieth-century England, among other times and places, 'reference groups tend to be closely circumscribed at all levels of society except under some abnormal stimulus'. But his discussion is not of much help in answering it.

---

[1] Cf. Margaret Stacey, *Tradition and Change: a Study of Banbury* (Oxford, 1960), pp. 146-7.
[2] 'Social stratification: a rejoinder to Mr Ingham', *Sociology*, 4 (1970), 246-8.

INDEX